SITUATIONAL FUNCTIONAL JAPANESE

VOLUME 3: NOTES
SECOND EDITION

TSUKUBA LANGUAGE GROUP

BONJINSHA CO.,LTD.

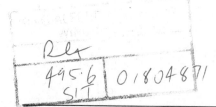
Published and distributed in Japan by BONJINSHA Co., Ltd.,
1F Ryōshin Hirakawachō Building, 1-3-13, Hirakawa-cho, Chiyoda -ku, Tokyo
Telephone 03-3472-2240
Printed in Singapore.

First edition, 1992
Second edition, 1994   ISBN4-89358-296-8 C3081

CONTENTS

TABLE OF CONTENTS

Conversation Notes

⟨General Information⟩	⟨Strategies⟩
1. Invitation cards	S-1. How to invite someone to go somewhere
	S-2. How to accept an invitation
	S-3. How to decline an invitation
1. Use of **Keego** on the telephone	S-1. How to ring someone at home
	S-2. How to ask to speak to the person you want
	S-3. How to arrange to ring again
	S-4. How to leave a message
	S-5. How to end a conversation —4. On the phone
	S-6. How to pass on a message
1. The Japanese house	S-1. How to start a conversation —7. Visiting
2. Bowing	S-2. How to express praise
3. Giving a present	S-3. How to end a conversation —4. Visiting
4. Meals	
5. The Japanese bath	
1. Vocabulary used to explain a procedure: for a photocopier, cooking recipe, etc.	S-1. How to start a conversation —8. Creating an opening
	S-2. How to explain a procedure
	S-3. How to ask for something to be done for you —2. In a casual way
	S-4. How to express an opinion

B. Conversation

Conversation Notes

⟨General Information⟩	⟨Strategies⟩
1. Refuse collection 2. Refering to people	S-1. How to complain S-2. How to express anger S-3. How to admit a mistake S-4. How to apologize —2.

1. Etiquette for visiting
   a sick person
2. Condolences and
   Celebration
	S-1. How to start a conversation —9.
	      Visiting a sick person
	S-2. How to give a present
	S-3. How to ask about the patient's
	      condition: symptoms, progress, etc.
	S-4. How to cheer up the patient
	S-5. Asking someone to be more careful

1. Expressions of apology	S-1. How to start a conversation —10.
	      Making a request
	S-2. How to make a request
	S-3. How to refuse a request politely
	S-4. How to withdraw a request that is
	      refused
	S-5. How to persuade someone to accept
	      your request

1. Useful information for planning a trip 2. Japanese inns	S-1. How to make a proposal S-2. How to voice disagreement S-3. How to support someone's view S-4. How to ask for someone's approval S-5. How to avoid a definite statement

B. Conversation

This volume is the third of the three volume work,"Situational Functional Japanese". Preliminary explanation may be found in "How to Use This Book" in Volume 1. The table of contents of Volume 1 and 2 is shown below.

Conversation Notes

⟨General Information⟩	⟨Strategies⟩
1. Formal introductions 2. Addressing people 3. Short questions and responses 4. Aizuchi	S-1. How to start a conversation —1. 　　At a party S-2. How to introduce yourself or others S-3. How to end a conversation —1. 　　After a meeting
1. Post office services in Japan 2. Letters and postcards 3. Paying and receiving money	S-1. How to start a conversation —2. 　　On the street S-2. How to start a conversation —3. 　　Introducing a request S-3. How to send mail at the post office S-4. How to buy something at the post office
1. At a restaurant 2. Expressions used in restaurants and shops 3. Fast food shops	S-1. How to ask for something S-2. How to give and receive something S-3. How to order S-4. How to deal with problems in a restaurant S-5. How to pay the cashier
1. Location	S-1. How to start a conversation —4. 　　Introducing a question S-2. How to ask the whereabouts of things/ people S-3. How to get something you didn't catch S-4. How to confirm information —1. S-5. How to gain time to collect your thoughts S-6. How to end a conversation —2. After asking a question

B. Conversation

Conversation Notes

〈General Information〉	〈Strategies〉
1. Katakana words	S-1. How to introduce a main topic —1. S-2. How to ask information about a word S-3. How to make sure you have understood S-4. How to end a conversation —3. When the speaker does not give the required explanation
1. Office instructions 2. Delivery service	S-1. How to introduce a main topic —2. S-2. How to ask for instructions S-3. How to correct others' mistakes S-4. How to ask for advice implicitly S-5. How to give an alternative
1. Telephones 2. Telephone numbers	S-1. How to ask for a telephone number S-2. How to make a telephone call S-3. How to deal with a wrong number S-4. How to introduce a question politely S-5. How to ask about office hours S-6. How to make an appointment
1. Relations between seniors and juniors in Japan 2. A request for leave of absence	S-1. How to start a conversation —5. Asking for permission S-2. How to introduce a main topic —3. S-3. How to ask permission S-4. How to give a warning

B. Conversation

Conversation Notes

〈General Information〉	〈Strategies〉
1. Hospitals in Japan	S-1. How to explain your symptoms
2. Procedures in a hospital	S-2. How to consult a doctor
3. Common phrases used by a doctor	S-3. How to ask for instructions on taking a medicine
4. Medicine	

1. Department stores in Japan	S-1. How to find what you want
2. Expressions used in a department store	S-2. How to ask for advice
3. Colours, patterns, sizes of clothes	S-3. How to decline politely

1. At a bookshop	S-1. How to ask for something to be done for you —1.
2. Casual introductions	S-2. How to order a book
	S-3. How to cancel your order

1. Location and landmarks	S-1. How to ask for directions
	S-2. How to give directions
	S-3. How to go by public transport
	S-4. How to confirm information —2.

B. Conversation

Conversation Notes

⟨General Information⟩	⟨Strategies⟩
1. Introductions —2. 2. Building a relationship in a conversation	S-1. How to apologize and give an excuse S-2. How to confirm what you heard from someone S-3. How to bring up the main topic S-4. How to make and accept an offer S-5. How to express modesty
1. The lost-and-found office 2. Shape, colour and size	S-1. How to enquire about something you left behind S-2. How to answer questions S-3. How to confirm information —3. S-4. How to describe something S-5. How to express one's feelings
1. University libraries	S-1. How to start a conversation —6. After not having seen each other for a long time S-2. How to talk about other people S-3. How to ask for advice on books S-4. How to thank for/decline offers of help S-5. How to ask how long you can borrow something
1. Using a taxi	S-1. How to propose a joint course of action S-2. How to substantiate a point with reasons S-3. How to call a taxi by phone S-4. How to explain where you are S-5. How to give instructions in a taxi

B. Conversation

Abbreviations and Notations

This is a list of main symbols used in this book:

🐟 (fish symbol)	discourse particles
🐟 (fish symbol)	structure particles
∞ (loop symbol)	connective particles
▼	Be careful!
○	correct
✕	wrong
[N]	noun
[A]	-i adjective
[NA]	na adjective
[V]	verb
[V(base)]	verb base
[V-(r)u]	-(r)u form of verb
[V-te]	-te form of verb
[V-ta]	-ta form of verb
[V-nai]	-nai form of verb
[V-nakatta]	-nakatta form of verb
《+を verbs》	verb with を (object particle)
《-を verbs》	verb without を (object particle)
|S|	sentence
⇨	Refer to
GN	Grammar Notes
CN	Conversation Notes
lit.	literally
🅴	formal/polite speech
🅲	casual/plain speech
⬆	speaking to a Higher
⬇	speaking to a Lower
➡	speaking to an Equal
♂	spoken by male
♀	spoken by female

友だちを誘う
とも　　　　さそ
Inviting a friend

OBJECTIVES:

GRAMMAR

I. ほしい: *want (something)*
II. ～てほしい: *want to get something done*
III. ～そうだ〈1〉: *looks (like)～*
IV. Passive sentences
V. 何でも，だれでも，どこでも，いつでも:
なん
＜question word ＋ でも＞

CONVERSATION

＜General Information＞

1. Invitation cards

＜Strategies＞

S-1. How to invite someone to go somewhere
S-2. How to accept an invitation
S-3. How to decline an invitation

Characters ：Lisa Brown, Tanaka(田中)，Suzuki(鈴木)

Situation ：Suzuki-san has invited Lisa-san and Tanaka-san to a concert. Tanaka-san can go but Lisa-san can't, because her professor has asked her to check a letter for him.

Flow-chart ：

```
┌─────────────────────────┐
│  Asking if s/he is free  │
└─────────────────────────┘
             ↓
┌─────────────────────────┐
│   Making the invitation  │
└─────────────────────────┘
      ↓              ↓
┌──────────────────┐ ┌──────────────────┐
│ Accepting the    │ │ Declining the    │
│ invitation       │ │ invitation       │
└──────────────────┘ └──────────────────┘
             ↓
┌─────────────────────────┐
│   Changing the topic     │
└─────────────────────────┘
             ↓
┌─────────────────────────┐
│   Selling the tickets    │
└─────────────────────────┘
```

―研究室で―

鈴　木：ねぇ、今度の日曜日ひま。
田　中：とくに、予定はないんですけど、何か。
鈴　木：クラブのコンサートがあるんだけどさ。
田　中：ええ。
鈴　木：よかったら、リサさんと二人で来ない。
リ　サ：あら、クラブって何やってるんですか。
鈴　木：合唱部なんだ。

田　中：えっ。鈴木さんって、歌、上手なんですか。
鈴　木：上手ってほどじゃないけど、好きなんだ。
田　中：ふうん。
鈴　木：ぜひ、来てほしいんだけど。
田　中：おもしろそうね。行ってみようかしら。

　　　　　　＊　　　　＊　　　　＊

鈴　木：リサさんは、どう。
リ　サ：行きたいけど、今度の日曜でしょう。
鈴　木：うん。6時から。
リ　サ：日曜の夜は、ちょっと…。

鈴　木：だめ。

リ　サ：ええ、もっと、早くわかってたら、ことわれたんですけど。

鈴　木：何かあるの。デート。

リ　サ：いいえ、先生に翻訳のチェックをしてほしいって頼まれてるんです。

鈴　木：ああ、そう。

　　　　残念だな。じゃ、この次は。

リ　サ：いつですか。

鈴　木：来月の19日、6時から。

リ　サ：ええ。じゃ、この次はぜひ。

　　　　　＊　　　　＊　　　　＊

田　中：あのう、山下君とアニルさんも誘ってもいいでしょうか。

鈴　木：もちろん。かまわないよ。

田　中：じゃ、あした、都合を聞いてみますから。

鈴　木：じゃ、切符3枚ね。

田　中：ええ。

鈴　木：1枚600円なんだ。

田　中：えっ。買うんですか。

鈴　木：お金の方は、いつでもいいからね。

Report

＜鈴木さんの日記＞

　今度の日曜に合唱部のコンサートがある。リサさんに来てほしいと思って誘ったが、先生に頼まれている仕事があるからとことわられた。残念だが、しかたがない。来月のコンサートには、来られると言った。日曜のコンサートには田中さんがアニルさんと山下君といっしょに来てくれると言った。切符が3枚売れてほんとうによかった。

3

New Words and Expressions

Words in the conversation

今度	こんど	next time
ひま		free time
予定	よてい	schedule
とくに		especially
クラブ		club
コンサート		concert
合唱部	がっしょうぶ	chorus club
歌	うた	song
好き	すき	like
ふうん		Is that so?
ぜひ		by all means
おもしろい		interesting
ことわる		to refuse, to reject
デート		date
翻訳	ほんやく	translation
チェック		check
頼む	たのむ	to ask
残念だ	ざんねんだ	What a pity
いつ		when
来月	らいげつ	next month
誘う	さそう	to invite
都合	つごう	convenience, availability
切符	きっぷ	ticket
～枚	まい	counter for tickets

＜Expressions in the conversation＞

クラブのコンサートがあるんだけどさ。

> さ serves to prompt the listener to react by giving Aizuchi etc. Note that さ is only used between close friends and should not be used to a Higher.

鈴木さんって歌、上手なんですか。　　　*Are you good at singing?*

The difference between 「鈴木さんって歌、上手なんですか。」 and 「鈴木さんは、歌、上手なんですか。」 is that the former indicates surprise at learning that Suzuki is good at singing, whereas 「鈴木さんは、歌、上手ですか。」 simply asks for information.

上手ってほどじゃないけど、　　　*I'm not that good, but...*
　　　c.f. **それほどでもない**　　　*Not that much, Not really.*

来てほしいんだけど。　　　*I'd like you to come to the concert.* ⇨GNⅡ

おもしろそうね。　　　*It looks interesting.* ⇨GNⅢ

行きたいけど、今度の日曜日でしょう。↗　　　*I want to go but it will be on next Sunday, won't it?*

　　　〜でしょう ⇨L19GNⅠ

先生に翻訳のチェックをしてほしいって頼まれているんです。
　　　　My teacher asked me to check his English translation.

　　　頼まれる is passive ⇨GNⅣ

かまわないよ。　　　*That's OK.*

<Expressions in the report>

しかたがない　　　*It can't be helped.*

Grammar Notes

I. ほしい: *want (something)*

Examples

① 小さい車がほしいです。　　　　　　*I want a small car.*
　　ちい　くるま

② 大きい車はほしくないです。　　　　*I don't want a big car.*
　　おお

③ 鈴木さんは車がほしいと言っています。　*Suzuki-san says he wants a car.*
　　すず　　　　　　　　　　　　　い

【*Explanation*】

ほしい is used to indicate that you want something:

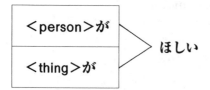

→（私が）車がほしい。　　　　　*I want a car.*
　　わたし

私が is often omitted because ほしい always expresses the subject's wishes.

Note that ほしい indicates that you want a THING (rarely, a person), whereas [V (base)] たい (⇨L7GN I) expresses the wish to DO something; look at the difference between the sentences below:

　　a. 車がほしい。　　　　　　　*I want a car.*
　　　くるま

　　b. 車が買いたい。　　　　　　*I want to buy a car.*
　　　　か

ほしい inflects like any -i adjective, so you simply add です to get the polite form:

6

		Non-past	Past
Positive	Plain	ほしい	ほしかった
	Polite	ほしいです	ほしかったです
Negative	Plain	ほしくない	ほしくなかった
	Polite	ほしくないです ほしくありません	ほしくなかったです ほしくありませんでした

To convey your wishes in a less direct way, **ほしいんですが** is used:

1. 申し込み用紙がほしいんですが。
　　　もう　こ　ようし
　I'd like an application form.

To convey someone else's wishes, add **と言っています** *to say, to be saying* as in ③
　　　　　　い
and the sentence below:

2. アニルさんはビデオがほしいと言っています。

　Anil-san says he wants a video.

Ⅱ. 〜てほしい: *want to get something done*

Examples

① **あした東京に行ってほしいんですが。**
　　　　とうきょう　い
I want you to go to Tokyo tomorrow.

② **田中さんが翻訳をチェックしてほしいと言っています。**
　　た なか　　ほんやく
Tanaka-san says she wants (you/me/us/someone) to check her translation.

【*Explanation*】

　　To indicate that you want someone to do something for you, attach **ほしい** to the
-te from of a verb:
　　[V-te] ほしい takes the following structure.

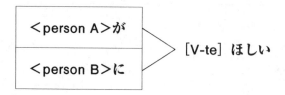

→ 私_{わたし}があなたに東京_{とうきょう}に行_いってほしい。
I want you to go to Tokyo.

→ 私_{わたし}があなたに翻訳_{ほんやく}をチェックしてほしい。
I want you to check my translation.

It is possible to omit **私が** and even **あなたに** because [V-te] **ほしい** is most commonly used to indicate something that the subject (which is often the speaker) wants the listener to do.

[V-te] **ほしい** alone expresses your wishes in a fairly strong and direct way, so it is often advisable to add **んですが** or **んですけど** to [V-te] **ほしい** to soften its impact. See ① and the sentence below:

1. ちょっと手伝_{てつだ}ってほしいんですが。   *I'd like you to help.*

2. 静_{しず}かにしてほしいんだけど。   *I'd like you to be quiet.*

Look at the following illustrations; can you tell who will go to Tokyo?

(1)

東京に行きたいです。

(2)

東京に行ってほしいです。

[V-te] **ほしい** is very similar in meaning to [V-te] **ください**, but whereas [V-te] **ほしい** conveys a wish, [V-te] **ください** indicates a request.

GN

a. 住所を教えてほしいんですが。　*I'd like you to give me your address.*
じゅうしょ　おし

b. 住所を教えてください。　*Give me your address, please.*

To convey someone else's wishes, add と言っています to [V-te] ほしい, as in ②
い
and the sentence below:

3. 田中さんがあした6時に来てほしいと言っています。
たなか　　　　　　じ　き
   Tanaka-san says she wants (you/me/us) to come at six tomorrow.

Instead of [V-te] ほしい, you can also use [V-te] もらいたい／いただきたい;
both are more polite than [V-te] ほしい.

4. 住所を教えてもらいたいんです。
   I'd like you to give me your address.

5. 翻訳のチェックをしていただきたいんですが。
   ほんやく
   I wonder if you could check my translation.

6. 田中さんがあした6時に来てもらいたいと言っています。
   Tanaka-san says she would like (you/me/us) to come at six tomorrow.

Ⅲ. ～そうだ〈1〉: *looks (like)*～

Examples

① このケーキはおいしそうですね。
   This cake looks delicious.

② A：こんにちは。元気そうですね。
   げんき
   Hello. You look well.

   B：ええ、おかげさまで。
   Thank you.

③ 雨が降りそうですから、かさを持っていったほうがいいですよ。
   あめ　ふ　　　　　　　　　　　　　　　も
   It looks like rain. You'd better bring an umbrella.

④ ドルが上がりそうです。
   あ
   The dollar looks like it will go up.

9

【*Explanation*】

1. Use of ～そうだ

Look at picture (1). The cake looks delicious, doesn't it? (But not having tasted it, you don't know if it really is.) In picture (2), the book looks as though it might fall off the desk any moment (but again, you don't know for sure).

(1)   (2)

To express this kind of unconfirmed impression, ～そうだ (politely, ～そうです) is used. You can therefore describe Picture (1) and (2) as:

(1) → **このケーキはおいしそうです**。

This cake looks delicious.

(2) → **本が落ちそうだ**。
ほん　　お
The book looks like it's about to fall off.

そうだ is attached to an adjective or a verb base as follows.

[V]	Group I	降る → 降り → 降りそうだ ふ
	Group II	落ちる → 落ち → 落ちそうだ お
	Group III	来る → 来 → 来そうだ く　　き　　き する → し → しそうだ
[A]		おいしい → おいし → おいしそうだ
[NA]		元気だ → 元気 → 元気そうだ げん き

10

GN

Note that **いい** or **よい** becomes **よさそうだ**, and **ない**, **なさそうだ**:

1. **この辞書がよさそうです。**
   じしょ
   This dictionary looks like it's good.

2. **この店には日本語の辞書はなさそうです。**
   みせ　　にほんご
   There don't seem to be any Japanese dictionaries in this shop.

〜そうだ can also be used after negative forms as follows.

おいしくない
↓

このケーキはおいしくなさそうです。

This cake looks like it isn't delicious.

便利じゃない
べんり
↓

この機械はあまり便利じゃなさそうです。
きかい

This machine looks as though it's not very useful.

Negative verb sentences are formed as follows.

降りそうだ
ふ
↓

雨は降りそうに（も）ありません。
あめ

It doesn't look like it's going to rain.

2. 〜そうな／そうに

The **〜そうだ** ending behaves like a **na** adjective:

1. **アニルさんはおいしそうなケーキを食べています。**
   た
   Anil-san is eating a delicious-looking cake.

2. **この店にはおもしろそうな本がたくさんあります。**
   ほん
   There are many books which look interesting.

3. **学生たちは楽しそうに話をしています。**
   がくせい　　たの　　　はなし
   The studens look happy talking.

   (lit. The students are talking, looking happy.)

4. **学生たちはおいしそうにビールを飲んでいます。**
   の
   The students look like they are enjoying their beer.

Ⅳ. Passive sentences

When A does something to B, this can be described from two different angles:

(1) from the viewpoint of A, who performs the action (Active)

(2) from the viewpoint of B, who is at the receiving end of the action (Passive).

In the pairs of examples below, (2) are passive sentences:

Examples

①

1)

(1) **先生がリサさんをほめました。**
せんせい
The teacher praised Lisa-san.

2)

(2) **リサさんが先生にほめられました。**
Lisa-san was praised by the teacher.

②

1)

(1) **鈴木さんがリサさんのカメラをこわしました。**
すずき
Suzuki-san broke Lisa-san's camera.

2)

(2) **リサさんが鈴木さんにカメラをこわされました。**
Lisa-san had her camera broken by Suzuki-san.

In Japanese passive sentences, the subject is usually animate, and usually a person. We can distinguish two types of passive sentences, direct (①) and indirect passives (②).

GN

1. Direct passives

The direct passive is used when the actor directly affects the subject.

Active sentence

1) <u>先生が</u>　<u>リサさんを</u>　ほめました。
せんせい
The teacher praised Lisa-san.

↓

Passive sentence

2) <u>リサさんが</u>　<u>先生に</u>　　ほめられました。
Lisa-san was praised by the teacher.

The subject (which can be the speaker) is marked by the particle が (は when topicalized), and the person who performs the action by the particle に.

When the subject is the speaker, 私は is usually omitted.
わたし

Active verb forms are converted to passive forms.

Below are some examples of passive sentences:

1. リサさんは山下さんに映画にさそわれました。
やました　　　　えいが
Lisa-san was invited to the movies by Yamashita-san.

2. スミスさんは先生に翻訳を頼まれた。
ほんやく　たの
Smith-san was asked by his teacher to do a translation.

3. こんばん（私は）木村先生に食事にさそわれています。
きむら　　　しょくじ
I'm invited to dinner by Kimura-sensee this evening.

2. Indirect passives

An indirect passive sentence normally implies the subject's somehow being inconvenienced by the action of the verb. In ② (2), Lisa-san is inconvenienced by Suzuki-san's having broken her camera. Although Suzuki-san's action directly affects only the camera, Lisa-san, its owner, is affected indirectly.

Active sentence

1）鈴木さんが　リサさんの　カメラを　こわしました。
すずき

Suzuki-san broke Lisa-san's camera.

↓

Passive sentence

2）リサさんが　鈴木さんに　カメラを　こわされました。

Lisa-san had her camera broken by Suzuki-san.

In an indirect passive sentence, the person indirectly affected（who may be the speaker）becomes the subject（marked by **が** or **は**）, his/her belongings which were directly affected by the action are marked by **を**, and the person performing the action by **に**.

1. （私は）どろぼうにお金をとられた。
わたし　　　　　　　　かね

   I had my money stolen by a burglar.

2. （私は）友だちに試験を見られた。
   とも　しけん　み

   I was inconvenienced by my friend looking at my exam paper.

The following are also indirect passive sentences.

3. リサさんは雨に降られて困りました。
   あめ　ふ　　こま

   Lisa-san was inconvenienced because she was rained on.

4. （私は）ゆうべ友だちに来られて、勉強できませんでした。
   こ　　　　べんきょう

   A friend came last night, so I couldn't study.

	Passive verbs			
Ordinary verbs	Non-past pos.	Non-past neg.	Past pos.	Past neg.
Group Ⅰ	**-u → -areru**			
kaku　*to write* 書く	kakareru 書かれる	kakarenai 書かれない	kakareta 書かれた	kakarenakatta 書かれなかった
tanomu　*to request* 頼む	tanomareru 頼まれる	tanomarenai 頼まれない	tanomareta 頼まれた	tanomarenakatta 頼まれなかった
yobu　*to call* 呼ぶ	yobareru 呼ばれる	yobarenai 呼ばれない	yobareta 呼ばれた	yobarenakatta 呼ばれなかった
toru　*to take* とる	torareru とられる	torarenai とられない	torareta とられた	torarenakatta とられなかった
sasou　*to invite* さそう	sasowareru さそわれる	sasowarenai さそわれない	sasowareta さそわれた	sasowarenakatta さそわれなかった
Group Ⅱ	**-ru → -rareru**			
taberu　*to eat* 食べる	taberareru 食べられる	taberarenai 食べられない	taberareta 食べられた	taberarenakatta 食べられなかった
miru　*to see* 見る	mirareru 見られる	mirarenai 見られない	mirareta 見られた	mirarenakatta 見られなかった
homeru　*to praise* ほめる	homerareru ほめられる	homerarenai ほめられない	homerareta ほめられた	homerarenakatta ほめられなかった
Group Ⅲ				
kuru　*to come* 来る	korareru 来られる	korarenai 来られない	korareta 来られた	korarenakatta 来られなかった
suru　*to do* する	sareru される	sarenai されない	sareta された	sarenakatta されなかった
shitsumon suru 質問する　*to ask a question*	shitsumon sareru 質問される	shitsumon sarenai 質問されない	shitsumon sareta 質問された	shitsumon sarenakatta 質問されなかった

GN

15

Passive verbs behave like Group Ⅱ verbs:

さそわれる　　　　　　　　さそわれて
さそわれない　　　　　　　さそわれます
さそわれた
さそわれなかった

▼ TO BE AVOIDED! Here are examples of some common mistakes made by students of Japanese.

In Japanese passives the speaker appears as the subject, not as actor.

○　私はリサさんを映画にさそいました。

×　リサさんは私に映画にさそわれました。

Passives aren't used for mutually beneficial actions like 会う or 結婚する - unless you want to indicate that one of the people involved was inconvenienced!

○　山田さんは田中さんに会いました。

×　田中さんは山田さんに会われました。

3. A new type of Japanese passive

As we saw earlier, the subject in a Japanese passive sentence is usually animate; recently, however, the use of passives with inanimate subjects is on the increase, especially in the media:

1. この寺は1950年に建てられた。
   This temple was built in 1950.

2. きのう新型ロケットが打ち上げられました。
   A new type of rocket was launched yesterday.

3. 山川さんが首相に選ばれた。
   Yamakawa-san was elected prime minister.

V. 何でも，だれでも，どこでも，いつでも: ＜question word＋でも＞

GN

The combination ＜question word＞＋でもいい has the following meanings:

何 なに	what?		何でもいい なん	Anything will do.
だれ	who?		だれでもいい	Anyone will do.
どこ	where?	＋ でもいい	どこでもいい	Anywhere will do.
いつ	when?		いつでもいい	Anytime will do.
どちら	which?		どちらでもいい	Either will do.
どれ	which?		どれでもいい	Any (of these) will do.

1. A：何にしましょうか。
   なん
   What would you like?

   B：私は何でもいいです。
   わたし
   Anything will do for me.

2. リサさんは何でも食べます。
   た
   Lisa-san eats anything.

3. だれでもいいから、ちょっと来てください。
   き
   Anyone will do - come here (for a minute).

4. A：お金、いつ払いましょうか。
   かね　　　はら
   When should I pay the money?

   B：いつでもいいですよ。
   Anytime (will do).

Conversation Notes

<General Information>

1. Invitation cards

In Japan there are various parties, such as wedding ceremonies (結婚式), thank-you parties for teachers (謝恩会), social gatherings of academic societies, etc. A reply postcard is usually enclosed with the invitation card.

The examples show an invitation card and reply postcard for a thank-you party for the teachers of a university.

① **日時** *date*
　にちじ

② **場所** *place*
　ばしょ

③ *Would you be so kind and return the enclosed reply postcard by March 3, indicating whether you intend to attend our thank-you party for the teachers.*

梅の香がほのかに漂い、日々に陽の強まりを憶える頃となりました。私どもが学窓を巣立つ日も近づいて参りました。こうして卒業の喜びを迎えることができますのも、ひとえに先生・職員の皆様の温かいご指導によるものと卒業生一同深く感謝いたしております。

つきましては、ささやかではございますが謝恩の会を催したく存じますので、是非ご出席下さいますよう、ご案内申しあげます。

記

一、日　時　平成〇年三月二十五日（水）十七時～　①

一、場　所　松見グランドパレス　鳳凰の間　②
　　　　　　ＪＲ松見駅東口（徒歩五分）

平成〇年二月

松見大学
平成〇年度卒業生一同

恐れいりますが、三月三日までに同封葉書にて、ご都合をお知らせ下さいませ。　③

18

CN

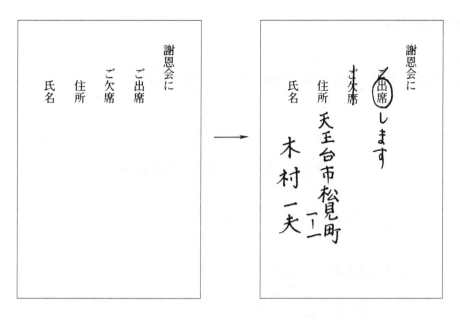

Reply postcard   Completed reply postcard

Replace 行 with 様

＜*Strategies*＞

S-1. How to invite someone to go somewhere

a. When you invite someone, you normally start off by asking if s/he is free:

① 🈁A：先生、今度の土曜日、お時間ありますか。
せんせい　こんど　どようび　　　じかん
Do you have time next Saturday?

B：ううん。↘ 授業があるんだ。
じゅぎょう
No, I have to attend a class.

② 🈁A：あした、｜時間ある。↗
　　　　　　　　｜ひま。↗

Do you have time tomorrow?

B：ええ。あしたは、何も予定がないけど。
なに　よてい
Yes, I don't have any plans.

③　A：山下君。きょうの午後、｜何か予定ある。↗ ⏬
やましたくん　　　　ごご　　　｜時間あるかな。↗
　　　　　　　　　　　　　　　　｜ひま。↗

Do you have any plans in the afternoon?

B：いいえ。何もありませんけど、何でしょうか。⏫
なん
No, I haven't. Why?

b. The following are commonly used when inviting someone to do something.

１）〈place/activity〉に｜行きませんか。🈁
　　　　　　　　　　　い
　　　　　　　　　　　｜行きましょう。🈁
　　　　　　　　　　　｜行かない。↗ 🈁
　　　　　　　　　　　｜行く。↗ 🈁

２）〈event〉を〈verb〉に｜行きませんか。🈁
　　　　　　　　　　　　｜行きましょう。🈁
　　　　　　　　　　　　｜行かない。↗ 🈁
　　　　　　　　　　　　｜行く。↗ 🈁

CN

In the model conversation Suzuki-san said 「よかったら、リサさんと二人で来ない」. This 来ない ↗ (negative question) does not have a negative meaning, but expresses an invitation. More politely, 来ませんか can be used:⇨L3GNV

① A：あした、私の家に ｜ 来ませんか。📱
　　　　　　　　　　　｜ 来ない。↗ 😀

　 B：はい。ありがとうございます。

② A：昼ご飯、いっしょに食べない。↗ 😀

　 B：うん。食べようか。😀

③ A：あした、映画見ない。↗ 😀

　 B：うん。行こうか。😀

＊Notes＊　　Note that 行く and 来る are used differently from English: 行く indicates motion away from the present location, whereas 来る indicates motion toward the speaker's home, or the present location.

① A：コンサートに ｜ 行きませんか。📱
　　　　　　　　　｜ 行かない。↗ 😀
　　　　　　　　　｜ 行く。↗ 😀

　 B：ええ。いいですね。↘
　　　That sounds good.

② A：あした、私の家に ｜ 来ませんか。📱
　　　　　　　　　　　｜ 来ない。↗ 😀
　　　　　　　　　　　｜ 来る。↗ 😀

　 B：ええ。ぜひ。
　　　Sure, I'd love to.

c. When you want to invite someone eagerly, you start off using ぜひ. ぜひ *by all means.*

ぜひ ｜ 来ていただきたいんですが。📱
　　　｜ 来てほしいんだけど。😀

21

S-2. How to accept an invitation

To accept an invitation, you can use the following:

①🈁A：**あした、映画に行かない。**↗
　　　How about going to the movies tomorrow?

　B：**ええ。いいわよ。**🈁♀　*Yeah, I'd like to.*
　　　うん。いいよ。🈁♂

②🈁A：**あした、映画に行きませんか。**
　　　Would you like to go to the movies tomorrow?

　B：**ええ。ぜひ。**　*Sure. I'd love to.*

よろこんで *happily, with pleasure* is derived from **よろこぶ**. When invited by a Higher, the above strategy is useful: thank for the offer, then accept (or decline).

③🈁A：**アニルさん。今週の日曜、私の家に来ませんか。**
　　　Would you like to come to my place on Sunday?

　B：**ありがとうございます。よろこんで。**
　　　Thank you very much. I'd love to.

S-3. How to decline an invitation

a. We have seen on various occasions that the Japanese avoid saying *No* directly and explicitly; this is especially so when turning down an offer or invitation:

①🈁A：**今度の土曜、映画に行きませんか。**

　B：**今度の土曜ですか。**

　A：**キネカで「レインマン」やってるんです。**

　B：**ううん。**↘ **土曜は、ちょっと。**↘

②🈁A：**今度の土曜、映画に行きませんか。**

　B：**今度の土曜。**↗

　A：**キネカで「レインマン」やってるんです。**

　B：**そうですね……。**

③ A：今度の土曜、映画に行かない。↗

B：今度の土曜。↗

A：キネカで「レインマン」やってるの。

B：行きたいけど……。

「土曜は、ちょっと」 'Saturday is a bit...' implies that Saturday is inconvenient. Expressions like ちょっと or そうですね are sufficient to make the listener aware that the offer/invitation cannot be accepted, and 「いいえ。だめなんです。」or 「いいえ。行けないんです。」 are therefore usually omitted. To a close friend, however, you can say directly 「いいえ、土曜はだめなんです。」

b. Giving a reason why you can't accept the invitation. We saw how to do this in lesson 16:

A：映画いかない。↗

B：うん、ちょっと。試験もあるし、お金もないし……。
Well, I have a test and I don't have any money and...

「〜し、〜し」or「〜から……」, combined with a hesitant tone, imply refusal. The second half of the sentence following 「〜し、〜し」or「〜から」 is often left unstated.

Note that these expressions like 「〜し、〜し」 cannot be used when addressing a superior.

A：アニルさん、今度の日曜に私の家に来ませんか。

(✕) B：すみません。日曜はちょっと。
友だちが国から来るし、いそがしいし。

(○) A：アニルさん、今度の日曜に私の家に来ませんか。

B：すみません。日曜はちょっと。
友だちが国から来ますので。

c. You invite your friend to do something, but s/he declines. What do you say next? See the examples below:

A：今度の土曜、コンサートに行かない。↗

B：うん、土曜はちょっと……。

A：だめ。↗ *impossible, bad .*

B：今度の土曜日は、保証人のお宅に行くことになってるから。

A：そう。じゃ、日曜は、どう。↗

By suggesting an alternative date or time, you can find out if your friend has any intention of accepting. If s/he still declines your invitation, finish the conversation with 「残念だな。じゃ、またいつか。」.

A：今度の土曜は、だめなんです。

B：じゃ、日曜は。

A：日曜も、ちょっと……。

B：残念だな。じゃ、またいつか。　*That's too bad. Well, may be next time.*

A：ええ。ごめんなさいね。

d. When you have to decline a Higher's invitation, first apologize using **すみません**, then explain why you can't accept his/her offer.

①　A：アニルさん、今度の日曜に私の家に来ませんか。⬇

　　B：すみません、先生。日曜の午後、国から友だちが来るので。⬆

②　A：あしたの昼、予定ある。↗⬇

　　B：あ、すみません。ちょっと。⬆

　　A：あしたね。松見大学から山田先生が見えるので、いっしょに昼ご飯でもと思ったんだけど。⬇
Prof. Yamada will come tomorrow, so I think we should have lunch with him.

　　B：申し訳ありません。⬆　*I'm sorry.*
実は、あした、ビザの延長で入管に行かなければならないんです。
Actually, I have to go to the immigration office to extend my visa.

　　A：あ、そうか。じゃ、しかたがないな。⬇

　　B：どうもすみません。⬆

第18課

電話をかける（3）：指導教官の家
でんわ　　　　　　　　しどうきょうかん　いえ
Phoning（3）: One's professor's home

OBJECTIVES:

GRAMMAR

Ⅰ. *Keego*「敬語」〈3〉: humble

Ⅱ. Reporting questions

〈question word〉〜か
〜かどうか ｝ 聞く／わかる:

ask/know ｛ 〈*when, where, etc.*〉〜
whether 〜

Ⅲ. 〜ことができる: *can* 〜

Ⅳ. 〜しか……ない: *only* 〜

Ⅴ. はじめ and はじめて: *the beginning/at first* and
for the first time

CONVERSATION

＜General Information＞

1. Use of *Keego* on the telephone

＜Strategies＞

S-1. How to ring someone at home

S-2. How to ask to speak to the person you want

S-3. How to arrange to ring again

S-4. How to leave a message

S-5. How to end a conversation ―4. On the phone

S-6. How to pass on a message

Model Conversation

Characters ：Yamashita(山下)， Kimura's wife(奥さん)， Prof. Kimura(木村)

Situation ：Yamashita-san phones Kimura-sensee. Kimura-sensee is not home, so he calls again later.

Flow-chart ：

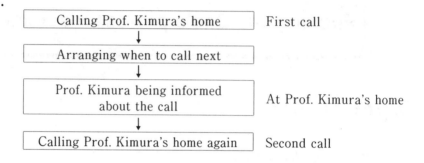

Calling Prof. Kimura's home	First call
↓	
Arranging when to call next	
↓	
Prof. Kimura being informed about the call	At Prof. Kimura's home
↓	
Calling Prof. Kimura's home again	Second call

（1）— 電話 1 （8：00 p. m.）—

山　下：もしもし。

奥さん：はい。

山　下：木村先生のお宅ですか。

奥さん：はい、木村でございます。

山　下：あ、あの、私、松見大学の山下と申しますが。

奥さん：ああ、山下さん。こんばんは。

山　下：こんばんは。
　　　　あの、先生、ご在宅でしょうか。

奥さん：すみません。まだ帰ってきてないんですよ。

山　下：あ、そうですか。

　　　　　　＊　　　　＊　　　　＊

山　下：あの、何時ごろお帰りになりますか。

奥さん：そうですね。10時ごろには帰ってると思いますけど。

山　下：あ、そうですか。
　　　　じゃ、10時ごろ、もう一度お電話してよろしいでしょうか。

奥さん：ええ、どうぞ。

山　下：じゃ、また、お電話いたします。

奥さん：申しわけございませんね。

山　下：じゃ、失礼します。

奥さん：ごめんください。

MC

（2）― 木村先生の家で ―

木　村：ただいま。

奥さん：お帰りなさい。

　　　　あ、8時ごろ山下さんから電話がありましたよ。

木　村：そう。何だって。

奥さん：10時ごろまた電話しますって。

木　村：あ、そう。

（3）― 電話2（10：10 p.m.）―

奥さん：はい。

山　下：もしもし、木村先生のお宅ですか。

奥さん：はい、木村でございます。

山　下：あ、あの、先ほどお電話した山下ですが。

奥さん：ああ、山下さんですね。

山　下：はい。

奥さん：ちょっとお待ちください。主人とかわりますから。

山　下：はい。どうも。

Report

＜山下さんの伝言＞

鈴木さんへ

　すみませんが、あしたのゼミには出席できません。

　タイの友だちがあした午前10時に成田に着くので、

　空港まで迎えに行きます。

　木村先生に電話で事情をお話ししたら、ぼくの発表は

　来週の月曜日にかえてくださいました。

　先生は、「あしたは鈴木さんに発表してもらおう。」

　とおっしゃっていましたので、よろしくお願いします。

　　　　　　　　　　　　11.7. 3:00 p.m.　　　　山下

New Words and Expressions

Words in the conversation

奥さん	おくさん	someone else's wife
お宅	おたく	someone else's home
申す	もうす	*to be called*, humble for 言う
ご在宅	ございたく	*to be at home* 🔊
いたす		*to do; humble for* する
家	いえ	*home, house*
先ほど	さきほど	*a little while ago* 🔊
主人	しゅじん	*my husband*
か（代）わる		*to put someone else on the phone*

＜Expressions in the conversation＞

もしもし。 *Hello?* ⇨L7CN S-2

木村先生のお宅ですか。 *Is that Prof. Kimura's home?*

〜のお宅ですか is used to check that you are connected correctly. ⇨CN S-1

木村でございます。 *Kimura speaking.* 🔊

The taker of a phone call usually identifies him/herself using the very formal 〜でございます rather than 〜です. ⇨GN I, L10CN2d

山下と申しますが。 *This is Yamashita speaking.* 🔊

The caller usually announces his/her name using the very formal 〜と申しますが rather than 〜ですが. ⇨GN I, CN S-1

ご在宅でしょうか。 *Is (〜) home?* 🔊

For private calls, this expression can be used instead of いらっしゃいますか, which is more common for business calls. ⇨CN S-2

10時ごろには *by about 10 o'clock*

お電話してよろしいでしょうか。 *Do you mind if I ring?* 🔊

In formal speech, よろしい is used instead of いい to ask permission. Besides 〜てよろしい, 〜てもよろしい can also be used. ⇨L8GN Ⅶ

28

申しわけございませんね。↘ *I am so sorry.* 🈁
もう
    申しわけございません or **申しわけありません** are very formal ways of saying sorry. ⇨L21CN S-2

    ね ↘ can be added to an apology to give it a friendly tone; it must not be used to a Higher.

ごめんください。 *Good bye.* ⇨CN S-5
    Like **失礼します**, this is a formal good bye; **ごめんください** is also used as
しつれい
a greeting when visiting someone. ⇨L19CN S-1

ただいま。 *I've just come back!* ⇨L19CN2

お帰りなさい。 *Welcome home!* ⇨L19CN2
かえ

何だって。↗ *What did he say?* 🥴
なん
    「**何て言ってた。↗**」 is often said like this.
い

主人とかわりますから。 *I will call my husband for you,*
しゅじん *(so wait a moment, please.)*

Words in the report

伝言	でんごん	message
出席する	しゅっせきする	to attend, to be present
タイ		Thailand
午前	ごぜん	in the morning, ⟨time⟩ a.m.
成田	なりた	Narita (airport)
空港	くうこう	airport
迎える	むかえる	to see, to welcome
事情	じじょう	circumstances
発表	はっぴょう	presentation
来週	らいしゅう	next week
月曜日	げつようび	Monday
か（変）える		to change
おっしゃる		to say; honorific for 言う

Grammar Notes

I. *Keego* 「敬語」〈3〉: humble

Examples

① A：いつ日本にいらっしゃいましたか。　*When did you come to Japan?*

　　B：先月まいりました。　　　　　　*I came last month.*

② お荷物をお持ちしましょうか。　　　*Shall I hold/carry your baggage?*

【*Explanation*】

Keego 「敬語」 can be divided into honorific and humble expressions. We learned about honorifics in Lessons 9 and 10, so let's look at humble expressions here.

Recall that honorific forms are used when the subject is someone else (including the listener); in contrast, humble expressions are used when you, the speaker (or a member of your family) are the subject.

先生：ケーキ、食べますか。　　*Will you have some cake?*

鈴木：はい、いただきます。　　*Yes, please (I will).*

ケーキ、食べますか。

はい、いただきます。

Suzuki-san answers with いただく (a humble form of 食べる) to refer to his own action of eating because he is speaking to a Higher (Kimura-sensee). The same speaker would use honorific forms when referring to Kimura-sensee's actions, so both honorific and humble have essentially the same purpose of expressing social status difference by elevating the status of the listener (honorific) or lowering that of the speaker (humble).
⇨L9GN VI, 10GN VII

30

GN

	Subject	Verb
Keego 敬語	listener/third person （higher social status） 木村先生は <small>き むらせんせい</small>	honorific verbs めしあがります
	speaker/ingroup 私は <small>わたし</small>	humble verbs いただきます
Normal polite	speaker/listener/other person 田中さん／私は <small>た なか</small>	〜ます 食べます <small>た</small>

1. Humble verbs

There are two types of humble verbs, regular and irregular.

1） <u>Regular humble verbs</u> are formed in the following way:

　＊ Group Ⅰ, Ⅱ verbs

> お ＋ ［V(base)］ ＋ する／します
> 　　　　　　　　　　いたす／いたします

持つ → お持ちする／お持ちします
<small>も</small>
話す → お話しする／お話しします
<small>はな</small>

1. 荷物をお持ちします。
<small>に もつ</small>
   I will hold/carry your baggage.

2. ちょっとお話ししたいことがあるんですが。
   There's something I'd like to talk to you about.

3. ここでお待ちします。
<small>ま</small>
   I will wait for you here.

4. A：駅までお送りしましょうか。
<small>えき　　　おく</small>
   Shall I take you to the station?

   B：ええ、お願いします。
<small>ねが</small>
   Yes, please.

2）**Irregular humble verbs** are mostly used for verbs which have no regular humble forms:

いる	*to stay*	おる／おります
行く 来る	*to go* *to come*	まいる／まいります
する	*to do*	いたす／いたします
～する		ご／お　～　する／します ご／お　～　いたす／いたします ex.　ご説明します　　　　*to explain* 　　　お電話いたします　　*to phone*
食べる 飲む	*to eat* *to drink*	いただく／いただきます
見る	*to see*	はいけんする／はいけんします
会う*	*to meet*	お目にかかる／お目にかかります
聞く* 訪ねる	*to ask* *to visit*	うかがう／うかがいます
言う	*to say*	もうす／もうします

＊Both irregular and regular humble verbs can be used for 会う, 聞く and 訪ねる.

5.　A：もしもし、道子さんはいらっしゃいますか。
　　　Hello, is Michiko-san home?

　　B：いえ、いまおりませんが。
　　　No, she isn't here at the moment.

6.　ちょっとうかがいますが、神戸大学はどちらでしょうか。
　　Excuse me (lit. May I ask), where is Kobe University?

7.　あしたお目にかかりたいんですが。
　　I would like to see you tomorrow.

GN

8. **あした もう一度お電話します。**
   いちど　　　でんわ
   I will ring again tomorrow.

9. **では、はじめからご説明いたします。**
   せつめい
   All right, I'll explain from the beginning.

3) Note the following about the use of humble expressions.

Humble expressions are not used to refer to your own action if it is not directly related to the Higher (including the listener), as illustrated below:

鈴木さん	**友だち**	**木村先生**	**知らない人（小川さん）**
すずき	とも	きむらせんせい	し　　　　　おがわ
Suzuki-san	*Suzuki-san's friend*	*Suzuki-san's Higher*	*someone Suzuki-san doesn't know*

（1）**小川：図書館で本をお借りになりましたか。**
　　おがわ　としょかん　ほん　　か
Did you borrow a book from the library?

鈴木：はい、借りました。
　　　　　　　か
Yes, I did.

図書館で本をお借りになりましたか。　　はい、借りました。

33

（2）**小川**：**木村先生に本をお借りになりましたか。**
き むらせんせい　ほん　か
Did you borrow a book from Kimura-sensee?

鈴木：**はい、お借りしました。**
すずき
Yes, I did.

木村先生に本をお借りになりましたか。　はい、お借りしました。

(1) doesn't use a humble verb because borrowing a book from the library is purely Suzuki-san's personal concern and has no connection with other people (including the listener). In contrast, a humble verb is used in (2) because Suzuki-san has borrowed the book from Kimura-sensee, a Higher.

4） The following humble verbs are exceptional in that they are used for politeness regardless of any connection with others:

1. **あした東京へまいります。**
とうきょう
I'll go to Tokyo tomorrow.

2. **一日家におります。**
いちにちいえ
I'll be home all day.

3. **インドのアニルともうします。**
I'm Anil from India.

4. **木村でございます。**
I'm Kimura/Kimura speaking.

5. **客**　：**もっと大きいセーター、ありますか。**
きゃく
Do you have any bigger sweaters?

店員：**はい、こちらにございます。**
てんいん
Yes, right here, sir/madam.

6. **はい、じゃ、そういたします。**
Right, I'll do that.

GN

2. Polite and plain forms of honorific and humble verbs

Both honorific and humble verbs can be used in their polite and plain forms.

The polite form is usually used in formal conversation and the plain form in casual conversation. Compare the following *Keego* conversation about 木村先生:

1) Casual conversation between friends:

鈴木：**木村先生は、ケーキ、<u>めしあがる</u>。**　　*Does Kimura-sensee eat cake?*

友だち：**うん、<u>めしあがる</u>よ。**　　*Yes, he does.*

木村先生は、ケーキ、めしあがる。　　うん、めしあがるよ。

2) Formal conversation between two relative strangers:

小川：**木村先生は、ケーキ、<u>めしあがりますか</u>。** *Does Kimura-sensee eat cake?*

鈴木：**ええ、<u>めしあがります</u>。**　　*Yes, he does.*

木村先生は、ケーキ、めしあがりますか。　　ええ、めしあがります。

35

		Keego 「敬語」	
	Ordinary verbs	Honorific	Humble
Casual style （Plain form）	食べる　*to eat* 飲む　　*to drink*	めしあがる	いただく
Formal style （Polite form）	食べます 飲みます	めしあがります	いただきます

II. Reporting questions

〈question word〉〜か
〜かどうか 　} 聞く/わかる: *ask/know* { 〈*when, where, etc.*〉〜
whether〜

Examples

① 田中さんがいつ東京へ行くか聞きました。
I asked when Tanaka-san will go to Tokyo.

② 田中さんが東京へ行くかどうか聞きました。
I asked if Tanaka-san will go to Tokyo.

【*Explanation*】

1. Reporting questions with 聞く

For reporting someone else's question, two types of sentences are used in Japanese; the choice between them depends on whether the question asks for information or a choice between *Yes* and *No*.

To report an information-seeking question (a question sentence containing a question word), adapt the original question as follows:

1) To report a question containing ＜question word＞ ～か＋聞く as in ①.

〈actual question〉 鈴木：田中さんはいつ東京へ行きますか。
すずき たなか とうきょう い

↓ *When will Tanaka-san go to Tokyo?*

〈reporting〉 鈴木さんは田中さんがいつ東京へ行くか聞きました。
き

Suzuki-san asked when Tanaka-san will go to Tokyo.

いつ東京へ行きますか。

鈴木さんは田中さんがいつ東京へ
行くか聞きました。

Note that 田中さん（the subject of the question）, is now marked by が and that
行きます（the predicate of the question）, changes to the plain form.

2) To report a Yes/No question, ～かどうか聞く is used, as in ②.

〈actual question〉 鈴木：田中さんは東京へ行きますか。

↓ *Will Tanaka-san go to Tokyo?*

〈reporting〉 鈴木さんは田中さんが東京へ行くかどうか聞きました。

Suzuki-san asked if Tanaka-san will go to Tokyo.

東京へ行きますか。

鈴木さんは田中さんが東京へ行くか
どうか聞きました。

The person who was asked the question can be mentioned in either kind of reported question: (Recall that 聞く takes the particle に).

〈actual question〉:　　　　　　→　　〈reporting〉:

田中さんは東京へ行きますか。
Will Tanaka-san go to Tokyo?

鈴木さんはリサさんに
田中さんが東京へ行くか
どうか聞きました。
Suzuki-san asked Lisa if
Tanaka will
go to Tokyo.

2. Reporting questions with other verbs

<question word> ～か／～かどうか is also used with some other verbs such as わかる and 知っている:

1. 田中さんがどこにいるかわかりません。
   I don't know where Tanaka-san is.

2. 田中さんがうちにいるかどうかわかりません。
   I don't know whether Tanaka-san is at home.

3. だれがコンピュータを使ったか知っていますか。
   Do you know who used the computer?

4. 田中さんがコンピュータを使ったかどうか知っていますか。
   Do you know if Tanaka-san used the computer?

5. リサさんがいつ来るか教えてください。
   Please tell me when Lisa-san will come.

[V]	見る、見た、見ない 見た、見ている 見ていない、……		わかる 知っている 聞く 教える
[A]	安い 安かった 安くない 安くなかった		
[NA]	便利* 便利だった 便利じゃない 便利じゃなかった	か かどうか　＋	
[N]	休み* 休みだった 休みじゃない 休みじゃなかった		

＊Before **か**, **だ** is normally omitted.

Ⅲ. ～ことができる: *can* ～

Besides the potential forms we saw in Lesson 14, ～ことができる can also be used to express what one can do: ⇨L14GN I

1. アニルさんは日本語を話すことができます。
＝アニルさんは日本語が話せます。

Anil-san can speak Japanese.

2. 日本語で手紙を書くことができません。

I can't write a letter in Japanese.

3. Ａ：留学生は図書館で本を借りることができますか。

Can foreign students borrow books from the library?

Ｂ：ええ、できます。

Yes, they can.

Ａ：何日借りることができますか。

For how many days can they borrow books?

Ⅳ. ～しか……ない: *only*～

～しか……ない *only* is used with negative verbs only:

1. Ａ：３千円貸して。

Can you lend me 3000 yen.

Ｂ：うん、いいよ。
あっ、千円しか持ってない。

All right. Oops, I've only got 1000 yen.

2. あれ、ひとつしかない。

Oh, there is only one (candy).

GN

3. **ひらがなしか覚えていない。**
I can only remember Hiragana.

Recall that **だけ** （⇨L9GNⅦ） also means *only* or *just,* **だけ** is only used with positive verbs:

4. **千円だけ持っている。**
I have got just 1000 yen.

5. **ひとつだけある。**
There's just one (candy).

6. **ひらがなだけ覚えている。**
I only remember Hiragana.

The difference between **だけ** and **しか** is not great; **しか** implies *only... and nothing else,* and is therefore more exclusive than **だけ**.

 7. **千円しか持っていない。**　*I've only 1000 yen, that's all.*

8. **千円だけ持っている。**　*I have got just 1000 yen.*

しか replaces the particles **が** and **を**, but is added to others.

Ⅴ．はじめ and はじめて: *the beginning/at first* and *for the first time*

1. はじめ *the beginning, at first*
はじめ is grammatically a noun; it is used as follows:

1. **はじめからもう一度読んでください。**
Please read it once more from the beginning.

2. **来月のはじめに広島へ行きます。**
I'll go to Hiroshima at the beginning of next month.

3. <u>はじめに</u>デパートに行って、次にスーパーへ行ってみました。

I went to the department store first and to the supermarket next.

4. この本は<u>はじめ</u>はやさしいが、だんだんむずかしくなる。

The first part of this book is easy, but it gradually gets difficult.

5. さしみは<u>はじめ</u>は好きじゃありませんでしたが、いまは大好きです。

I didn't like sashimi at first, but now I like it very much.

2. はじめて *for the first time*

はじめ must not be confused with はじめて *for the first time* (as an experience) which is used as follows:

1. きのう<u>はじめて</u>さしみを食べました。

I ate sashimi for the first time yesterday.

2. Ａ：富士山ってきれいですね。

Mt. Fuji is beautiful, isn't it?

Ｂ：はじめてですか。

Is this your first time (you see/visit it)?

Ａ：いえ、2度目です。

No, it's my second time.

Conversation Notes

<General Information>

1. Use of *Keego* on the telephone

a. Speaker-listener relation

You will normally use **Keego** to an outgroup person (your senior, teacher, boss, customers and near-strangers). ⇨L9GNⅥ, L10GNⅦ, L18GNⅠ

① (A teacher is invited to a students' party on the phone.)

田中：先生、何時ごろ<u>いらっしゃいますか</u>。（honorific）⬆
たなか　せんせい　なんじ
What time will you come?

木村：７時ごろかな。
きむら　　じ
About 7:00.

田中：はい。じゃ、<u>お待ちしております</u>。（humble）⬆
　　　　　　　　　ま
Great, We'll be expecting you.

② (Two people talk about their first meeting on the phone.)

A：じゃ、１時ごろ<u>うかがいます</u>。（humble）⬆
　　　　　じ
I'll come around 1:00 then.

B：はい。<u>お待ちしております</u>。（humble）⬆
I'll be expecting you.

b. Relation with the person talked about

Keego about a third person can be also used in casual speech:

① (Two students talk about Prof. Kimura on the phone.)

山下：木村先生、何時ごろ<u>いらっしゃる</u>。↗（honorific）
　　　　　せんせい　なん
What time will Prof. Kimura get here?

田中：７時ごろって<u>おっしゃってた</u>よ。（honorific）
He said about 7:00.

If the person talked about in a formal situation belongs to the listener's group, **Keego** is used for both（even if the person talked about is a friend）. In the following example, Yamashita uses いらっしゃいますか（honorific）as **Keego** because Midori is the daughter of the listener.

②（Yamashita rings Midori's home and speaks to her mother.）

山下 ：みどりさん、<u>いらっしゃいますか</u>。（honorific）⬆
Is Midori in?

みどりの母：あ、いまちょっと出かけてますけど。
Sorry, she is out now.

When the person talked about belongs to your group, use **Keego** for the listener but not for the ingroup person（even if that person is your boss!）. The listener, however, may use **Keego** for the person talked about. In the following example, the secretary uses 外出しております（humble）as **Keego** for the customer, but not for her boss.

③（A customer rings an office and asks a secretary.）

customer：社長さん、<u>いらっしゃいますか</u>。（honorific）⬆
Is the chairman in?

secretary：もうしわけございません。
社長は、ただいま<u>外出しております</u>が。（humble）⬆
I'm sorry, he's out at the moment.

＜Strategies＞

S-1. How to ring someone at home

CN

When ringing a private number, it is usual to check that you dialed the right number with 〜さんのお宅ですか.

① 🈁山　下　：もしもし、木村先生のお宅ですか。
Hello, is that Prof. Kimura's residence?

木村夫人：はい、木村でございます。
Yes, this is Kimura.

After that, you give your name and, if necessary, any further appropriate information about yourself, using the expressions below:

〜ですが。　　　　　　　　*This is 〜.*
〜と申しますが。（polite）

② 先ほどお電話した山下ですが。
This is Yamashita. I called earlier.

③ 　私、松見大学の山下と申しますが。
My name is Yamashita from Matsumi University.

A telephone conversation is normally begun using formal expressions; once you know who you're talking to, you can exchange greetings appropriate to your relationship.

④ 🈁山　下　：あの、私、松見大学の山下と申しますが。

木村夫人：ああ、山下さん。こんばんは。

山　下　：こんばんは。

⑤（A and B are good friends. B: 👤）
　🈁山下：あの、山下ですが。

田中：ああ、山下さん。ひさしぶりね。元気。↗

山下：うん、なんとか。

S-2. How to ask to speak to the person you want

a. When you ring someone at home and someone else answers the phone, you can use the following expressions to ask for the person you want:

～さん	お願_{ねが}いします。
	いらっしゃいますか。　　　　（polite）
	いらっしゃいますでしょうか。（very polite）

ご在宅_{ざいたく}ですか can be used instead of いらっしゃいますか, but it sounds a little businesslike.

When ringing someone at home, the first name is often used.

① **みどりさん、いらっしゃいますか。**

May I speak to Midori-san?

If you don't know the first name or if you're not close, you can give some information to clarify whom you want:

② **松見大学_{まつみだいがく}の田中_{たなか}さん、いらっしゃいますでしょうか。**

May I speak to Tanaka-san, (a student) of Matsumi University, please?

Then the person on the phone will reply using いまかわりますから as follows:

③ **山下_{やました}　：あの、みどりさん、お願いします。**

みどりの母_{はは}：はい。
　　　　　　ちょっとお待_まちください。いまかわりますから。

Please wait a moment. I'll get for you.

If the person you want isn't at home, 出_でかけている or 帰_{かえ}って（きて）いない can be used in reply:

④ **山下_{やました}　：あの、みどりさん、いらっしゃいますか。**

みどりの母：あ、いまちょっと出かけてますけど。

Sorry, she is out now.

⑤ **山下_{やました}　：あの、木村先生_{きむらせんせい}、いらっしゃいますでしょうか。**

木村夫人_{ふじん}：すみません。まだ帰ってきてないんですが。

I'm sorry but he hasn't come home yet.

b. When ringing someone at the office, **お願いします** is often used to request the person you want. If necessary, give the person's full name and his/her department or position:

① 鈴　木　：宣伝部の石井 進さん、お願いします。
　　　　　　　May I speak to Mr. Susumu Ishii of the publicity department?

　　会社の人：はい。少々お待ちください。

When the person is a member of your family, you can not use **いらっしゃいますか** and **〜さん**.

② 木村夫人：木村の家内ですが、木村、お願いします。
　　　　　　This is Mrs. Kimura. May I speak to my husband?

　　鈴　木　：はい。少々お待ちください。

If the person you want isn't at her/his office, **席をはずしている** is often used in reply:

③ 鈴　木　：宣伝部の石井 進さん、お願いします。

　　会社の人：少々お待ちください。(Looking around)
　　　　　　　すみません。いまちょっと席をはずしてますが。
　　　　　　　I'm sorry but he is not at his desk just now.

When the person you want is a teacher in his/her office, *Keego* for the teacher is used in reply:

④ 木村夫人：木村の家内ですが、木村、お願いします。

　　鈴　木　：すみません。いまちょっと席をはずしていらっしゃいますが。

⑤ A：あの、木村先生いらっしゃいますか。

　　B：すみません。まだお見えになってませんが。
　　　　I'm sorry but he hasn't arrived yet.

Other expressions used in reply are as follows:

いま｜会議中｜です。　　*S/he is at a meeting now.*
　　　｜授業中｜　　　　*S/he is in class now.*

もうお帰りになりました。(honorific for もう帰りました)
　　　　S/he has gone home.

まだお見えになってません。(honorific for まだ来てません)

S/he has not come yet.

きょうはお休みです。　　　　 S/he is off today.

S-3. How to arrange to ring again

a. If the person you want is not at home, you can ask when s/he will be back using
お帰りになる（honorific for 帰る）:

何時ごろお帰り | ですか。
| になりますか。
| になるでしょうか。　　（polite）
| になりますでしょうか。（very polite）

What time will s/he be back?

The following expressions are often used in reply:

〈time〉ごろ | になると思いますが。　 *I think s/he'll be back around* 〜.
| 帰るって言ってましたけど。　 *S/he said s/he'll be back around* 〜.

〈time〉ごろには帰ってると思います。

I think s/he'll be back by 〜 *or so.*

きょうは遅くなるって言ってましたけど。

S/he said s/he'll be late coming home today.

ちょっとわからないんですが。

I'm sorry but I don't know.

After getting the information, you can indicate when you will call again:

〈time〉ごろ、またお電話 | します。
| いたします。（polite）

I'll call again around 〜.

You can also say そのころ instead of repeating the time indicated:

CN

① 山下　　：何時ごろお帰りになりますか。

みどりの母：10時ごろ帰るって言ってましたけど。

山下　　：あ、そうですか。
じゃ、そのころ、またお電話します。
I'll call again around that time.

Or you can ask superpolitely:

もう一度／また　お電話して（も）よろしいでしょうか。
Would it be all right to call again?

② 山下　　：あの、何時ごろお帰りになりますか。

木村夫人：そうですね。
10時ごろには帰ってると思いますけど。

山下　　：あ、そうですか。
じゃ、10時ごろまたお電話してよろしいでしょうか。

木村夫人：ええ、どうぞ。

If you don't know exactly when you can call again, you can simply say:

じゃ、また（あとで）お電話します。　　*I'll call again later.*

b. When ringing the office, use **もどる** instead of **帰る**. If the person you want is outgroup, use **おもどりになる**:

① A：あの、木村先生、いらっしゃいますでしょうか。

B：あ、いま、授業中なんですけど。

A：あ、そうですか。
何時ごろおもどりになりますか。
What time will he be back?

B：2時ごろになると思いますけど。

A：あ、そうですか。じゃ、そのころ、またお電話します。

B：はい。

When it becomes clear that the person hasn't come in yet, use **いらっしゃる／お見えになる**（honorific for **来る**）for an outgroup person:

② A：あの、木村先生、いらっしゃいますか。

B：すみません。まだお見えになってませんが。

A：何時ごろお見えになりますか。
What time do you expect him?

B：もうすぐ、いらっしゃると思いますけど。
He should be here shortly.

A：あ、そうですか。じゃ、またあとでお電話します。

B：はい。

S-4. How to leave a message

a. When you want the person to call you later, you can leave a message using **お電話 くださいとお伝えください** as follows:

① みどりの母：もうすぐ帰ってくると思いますけど。

　 山　下　：あ、そうですか。
　　　　　　　じゃ、すみませんが、お帰りになりましたら、お電話く
　　　　　　　ださいとお伝えください。
　　　　　　　Can she call me when she is back?

You can also specify a time:

② みどりの母：きょうは遅くなるって言ってましたけど。

　 山　下　：あ、そうですか。じゃ、すみませんが、あしたの午前中
　　　　　　　にお電話くださいとお伝えください。
　　　　　　　Can she call me tomorrow morning?

If the person you want is a member of your family, you'd say as follows:

③ 鈴　木　：いまちょっと席をはずしていらっしゃいますが。

　 木村夫人：じゃ、すみませんが、もどりましたら、家のほうに電話す
　　　　　　　るようにお伝えください。
　　　　　　　Could you please tell him to ring home when he is back?

＊NOTE＊　Generally in Japan, it is not polite to leave a message asking your teacher to return your call.

b. You can ask as follows to have a message taken:

伝言、お願い ｜ します。
｜ できますか。　　（polite）
｜ したいんですが。（polite）

May I please leave a message?

Then state your message:

（〈topic〉のことなんですが、）
〈message〉と ｜ 伝えてください。
｜ お伝えください。（polite）

Can you please tell him/her that ～.

① 山下　　：じゃ、すみませんが、伝言お願いできますか。
　　　　　　　　May I please leave a message?

みどりの母：はい、どうぞ。
　　　　　　　Yes, go ahead.

山下　　：あの、ゼミのことなんですが、あしたは中止になりましたとお伝えください。
　　　　　　　Could you please tell her that the seminar tomorrow has been cancelled?

If you are leaving a message for someone else, you can also use ～ので、よろしく.

② 鈴木　　：じゃ、すみませんが、伝言お願いします。

会社の人：はい、どうぞ。

鈴木　　：あしたの午後２時ごろそちらにうかがいますので、よろしくお伝えください。
　　　　　　　Could you please tell him that I will come to his office around 2:00 p.m. tomorrow?

S-5. How to end a conversation —4. On the phone

To end a telephone conversation, use 失礼します or ごめんください in formal
speech, and じゃ、また or どうも in casual speech.

① Ⓕ山　下　：じゃ、失礼します。

　　木村夫人：ごめんください。

② Ⓒ山　下：じゃ、また。

　　田　中：どうも。

When the person you want isn't in, you can end the conversation simply by saying
どうも失礼しました:

③　会社の人：もうお帰りになりました。

　　鈴　木　：あ、そうですか。どうも失礼しました。
　　　　　　　I see. Sorry for bothering you.

　　会社の人：いいえ。
　　　　　　　Not at all.

When asked if you want to leave a message, you can decline with いえ、けっこう
です and end the conversation: ⇨まとめ3BⅡ1

④　会社の人：何か伝言ございますか。
　　　　　　　Would you like to leave a message?

　　鈴　木　：いえ、けっこうです。どうも失礼しました。
　　　　　　　No, thank you. Sorry for bothering you.

　　会社の人：いいえ。

When you leave a message or make a request, end the conversation with よろしく
お願いします（Ⓕ）and よろしく（Ⓒ）.

⑤ Ⓕ山　下　：じゃ、よろしくお願いします。

　　木村夫人：はい。

⑥ Ⓒ山　下：じゃ、よろしく。
　　田　中：はい。

S-6. How to pass on a message

CN

You can pass on a telephone message as follows:

〈time〉、〈person〉から | 電話があったよ。　　　　🄲
　　　　　　　　　　　　 | 電話がありました（よ）。　🄹
　　　　　　　　　　　　 | お電話がありました（よ）。🄹

There was a telephone call from ＜person＞ for you at ＜time＞.

〈message〉 | って。　　　　　　🄲
　　　　　 | と言ってました。🄹

S/he said ＜message＞.

If the caller is an outgroup person, use とおっしゃってました.

① (A student gives a message to a teacher.)
　　🄹鈴木：2時ごろ奥さんからお電話がありました。
　　　　　　Your wife rang around 2:00.

　　木村：そう。何だって。
　　　　　What did she say?

　　鈴木：お宅に電話してくださいとおっしゃってました。
　　　　　She asked for you to call her at home.

　　木村：あ、そう。どうもありがとう。
　　　　　I see. Thank you.

② (Prof. Kimura's wife gives a message to Prof. Kimura.)
　　🄲木村夫人：8時ごろ山下さんから電話がありましたよ。

　　木　村　：そう。何だって。

　　木村夫人：10時ごろまた電話しますって。

　　木　村　：あ、そう。

ちょっとおもしろい話

　最近、留守番電話が多い。友だちの家に電話して、「ただ今留守にしております。ピーという音のあとに、お名前とご用件をお話しください。」などと言われると、困る。日本人でも、急に「一分間でメッセージをお願いします。」などと言われたら、なかなかうまく話すことができない。

　「ええっ、困ったな。あのう、田中ですけど、ええと、…」などと言って録音時間が終わる人、「何だよ、これ。」と、急に電話を切る人もいる。あとで相手がそんなメッセージを聞くと思うと、はずかしいので、自分が話すのはいやだが、人のメッセージを聞くのは楽しいし、便利だ。

　電話をををかけるときには、「留守番電話だったら、どう言おうか。」と考えてから、かけたほうがいいと思う。

＊留守番電話	answering machine
ただ今	at the moment
留守にする	to be out, to be not in
音	sound
用件	reason for calling
日本人でも、	even a Japanese
急に	suddenly
なかなか…できない	hardly can...
録音時間	recording time
電話を切る	to hang up
相手	the other party
はずかしい	shy, ashamed

54

第19課

訪問
ほうもん
Visiting

OBJECTIVES:

GRAMMAR

Ⅰ. ～だろう: *I suppose* ～, *probably*
Ⅱ. ～だろうと思う: *I think that probably* ～
Ⅲ. ～そうだ〈2〉: *I have heard that* ～
Ⅳ. ～つもりだ: *intend to* ～
Ⅴ. *Keego*「敬語」〈4〉: passive honorifics
Ⅵ. ～ながら:（doing something）*while*（doing
　　　　　　something else）
Ⅶ. The こ/そ/あ/ど system〈2〉:
　　こんな・そんな・あんな・どんな～…*sort of*～
Ⅷ. ～でも: ～ *or something*

CONVERSATION

＜General Information＞
1. The Japanese house
2. Bowing
3. Giving a present
4. Meals
5. The Japanese bath

＜Strategies＞
S-1. How to start a conversation —7. Visiting
S-2. How to express praise
S-3. How to end a conversation —4. Visiting

Model Conversation

Characters : Anil Sharma(シャルマ), Prof. Kimura(木村先生), Kimura's wife(奥さん)

Situation : Anil visits Prof. Kimura's home. Prof. Kimura and his wife entertain him lavishly and Anil has an enjoyable evening.

Flow-chart :

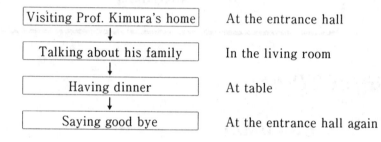

Visiting Prof. Kimura's home	At the entrance hall
↓	
Talking about his family	In the living room
↓	
Having dinner	At table
↓	
Saying good bye	At the entrance hall again

（1）—玄関で—

奥さん　：(Sound of chime) はい。
　　　　　あっ、シャルマさん、よくいらっしゃいました。
シャルマ：こんばんは。
奥さん　：こんばんは。どうぞお上がりください。
シャルマ：はい。失礼します。
奥さん　：外は寒かったでしょう。
シャルマ：ええ。
奥さん　：コート、おあずかりしましょう。
シャルマ：あ、どうもすみません。
奥さん　：どうぞ、こちらに。
シャルマ：はい、おじゃまします。

　　　　　＊　　　　＊　　　　＊

（2）― 客間で ―

奥さん　：シャルマさんは、お子さんいらっしゃるんですって。
シャルマ：ええ。
　　　　　（Showing a photo）まだ、小さいんですけど。
奥さん　：あら、かわいいわね。
シャルマ：はあ、どうも。
奥さん　：おいくつ。
シャルマ：8ヶ月なんです。
奥さん　：あ、そう。じゃ、会いたいでしょうね。
シャルマ：ええ。試験が終わったら、国へ帰るつもりなんですけど。
奥さん　：ああ、そうですか。

（3）― 食べながら ―

奥さん　：シャルマさん、お魚はだいじょうぶでしたね。
シャルマ：ええ。
奥さん　：じゃ、ごえんりょなくめしあがってくださいね。
シャルマ：はい、いただきます。
木　村　：シャルマ君、ビールは。
シャルマ：あ、すみません。お酒はちょっと……。
奥さん　：あ、じゃ、ジュースでもお持ちしましょう。
シャルマ：どうもすみません。

（4）― 帰る ―

シャルマ：先生、あの、そろそろ失礼します。
木　村　：きょうはもっとゆっくりしていってもいいんだろう。
シャルマ：ええ。でも、これからあしたの準備がありますから。
木　村　：ああ、そうか。それじゃ。
シャルマ：はい。
木　村　：母さん。シャルマさん、帰るって。
奥さん　：あら、もうそんな時間ですか。
シャルマ：ええ。きょうはほんとうにどうもごちそうさまでした。
奥さん　：また来てくださいね。
シャルマ：ええ。ありがとうございます。じゃ、失礼します。
奥さん　：おやすみなさい。
木　村　：おやすみ。

Report

　先日はご招待いただきありがとうございました。

　奥様の作られた家庭料理をいっしょにいただき、久しぶりに、楽しい時間をすごしました。４月になったら、家内をこちらに呼ぶつもりですから、今度は先生にも家内の作った料理をめしあがっていただきたいと思います。インドにもからくない料理がたくさんあります。

　今後の研究計画については、先生のご意見を参考にして、もう一度考えてみようと思っています。これからもどうぞよろしくお願いします。

　では、ほんとうにありがとうございました。奥様にもよろしくお伝えください。

　11月25日

アニル・シャルマ

木村先生

New Words and Expressions

Words in the conversation

訪問	ほうもん	*visiting*
玄関	げんかん	*entrance hall*
いらっしゃる		*to come, etc.*
		honorific for 来る／
		行く／いる
上がる	あがる	*to enter*
外	そと	*outside*
寒い	さむい	*cold*
コート		*coat*
あずかる		*to take*
ゆっくりする		*to stay longer*
客間	きゃくま	*guest room*
小さい	ちいさい	*small*
はあ		*yes*
かわいい		*cute*
いくつ		*How old?*
８ヶ月	はっかげつ	*8 months*
試験	しけん	*examination*
魚	さかな	*fish*
めしあがる		honorific for 食べる
ビール		*beer*
ジュース		*juice*
準備	じゅんび	*preparation*
時間	じかん	*time*
ほんとうに		*truly*

MC

59

＜*Expressions in the conversation*＞

よくいらっしゃいました。　　　　　　　　　*Welcome.*

　　＝**いらっしゃい。**（less polite）　**いらっしゃる** is honorific for **来る**

　　⇨CN S-1

　　In shops, 「**いらっしゃいませ。**」 is generally used.

こんばんは。　　　　　　　　　　　　　　　*Good evening.*

どうぞお上がりください。　　　　　　　　　*Please come inside.*

　　あがる implies taking off one's shoes and entering the house. When inviting

　　someone to enter a room, 「**お入りください。**」 is used.　⇨CN S-1

おじゃまします。　　　　　　　　　　　　　*lit. I'll disturb you.*

　　This expression is used when you enter someone's room, home, office, etc.

　　＝**失礼します。**⇨CN S-1

　① **おじゃましてもいいですか。**

　　　May I disturb you?

　② **おじゃましました。**

　　　Excuse me for having disturbed you.

　③ **大変おじゃましました。**

　　　I'm afraid I stayed rather too long.

　④ **おじゃまじゃなかったら、あしたうかがいたいんですが。**

　　　If it's not inconvenient, I'd like to visit you tomorrow.

お魚はだいじょうぶでしたね。　　　　　　*You can eat fish, can't you?*

　　～でしたね。（past tense）as opposed to **～ですね。** indicates that the

　　speaker has some previous knowledge as to whether Sharma can eat fish.

えんりょなくめしあがってくださいね。　　*lit. Please feel free to eat (lots).*

　　Used when offering food. A response is **それじゃ、えんりょなく** *I'll help*

　　myself then.　⇨CN4　**めしあがる**　⇨L13GN I

いただきます。　　　　　　　　　　　　*Yes, thank you. (lit. Thank you for this food*

　　　　　　　　　　　　　　　　　　　　I am about to eat.)

　　A greeting used before a meal.　⇨CN4

そろそろ失礼します。　　　　　　　　　　*I must get going.*

　　そろそろ literally means *gradually.*

① そろそろくらくなってきました。　*It's getting dark.*
② そろそろ行きましょう。　*Let's get going.*
③ もうそろそろ12時ですね。　*It's almost midday.*

きょうはもっとゆっくりしていってもいいんだろう。↗🕯

　　　　　　　　　　　　　　　　　You can stay longer, can't you?

cf. **ゆっくりしてください** means *Please make yourself at home.*

母さん。↗　　　　　　　　　　　　　*Dear.*
かあ

Usually（**お**）**母さん** is used not only to talk about someone else's mother, but also to address one's own mother or wife. In Japan, one does not call one's wife or husband darling, etc. Before having children, young couples usually address each other by their first names. Once they are parents, they often call each other **お母さん、ママ** or **お父さん、パパ**.
　　　　　　　　　　　　　　　　　とう

もうそんな時間ですか。　　　　　　　*Is it already that late?*
　　　じかん

ほんとうにどうもごちそうさまでした。　*Thank you for the wonderful meal/your hospitality.*

　　A greeting used after a meal. ⇨CN4

cf. **ごちそう**　　　　　　　　　　　*a treat, a feast*
　　ごちそうする　　　　　　　　*to treat someone to*（food）

おやすみなさい。／おやすみ。　　　　*Good night.*

Words in the report

先日	せんじつ	*the other day, a few days ago*
招待	しょうたい	*invitation*
奥様	おくさま	polite form for 奥さん
家庭料理	かていりょうり	*home cooking*
久しぶりに	ひさしぶりに	*after a long time*
楽しい	たのしい	*pleasant, happy*
すごす		*spend (time), pass (time)*
家内	かない	*my wife*
からい		*hot*
今後の	こんごの	*from now*
研究計画	けんきゅうけいかく	*research plan*
意見	いけん	*one's opinion*
参考	さんこう	*reference, consultation*
考える	かんがえる	*to think*

＜*Expressions in the report*＞

楽しい時間をすごしました。   *I had a pleasant time.*

これからもどうぞよろしくお願いします。   *Please do your best for me.*

奥様にもよろしくお伝えください。   *Give my best wishes to your wife.*
                                                                  Say hello to your wife.

Grammar Notes

Ⅰ. 〜だろう: *I suppose 〜, probably*

Examples

① あしたは雨でしょう。(↘)
It'll rain tomorrow.

② 松見公園はどこでしょうか。(↘)
Could you tell me where Matsumi Park is?

③ 疲れたでしょう／だろう。(↗)(↘)
You must be tired.

④ あの人は山田さんでしょう／だろう。(↗)
That man must be Yamada-san, right?

【*Explanation*】

でしょう (or だろう, the plain form of でしょう) basically means *probably is/was〜*, or *must be/have been〜*, expressing probability or conjecture. It can be used for both future and past events or actions, and has a variety of uses:

1. For yet unproved events/action

In ①, でしょう expresses uncertainty about the future; it is therefore often used in weather forecasts, although in this case the guessing is supported by evidence from satellites, etc.!

1. 台風はあしたの朝、東京を通過するでしょう。(↘)
The typhoon will probably pass through Tokyo tomorrow morning.

あしたは
台風でしょう。

2. For asking a question politely

As we saw earlier, (⇨L4CN S-2) ～でしょうか in ② gives a question a more polite ring than ～ですか.

1. **すみません、郵便局、どこでしょうか。**(↘)
   Excuse me, could you tell me where the post office is?

2. **家賃はいくらでしょうか。**(↘)
   Could you tell me how much the rent is?

郵便局どこで
しょうか。

3. To ask for confirmation

This doesn't indicate uncertainty but expresses empathy for the listener (③);

1. **疲れたでしょう。**(↘)／(↗)
   You must be tired.

2. **外は寒かったでしょう。**(↘)／(↗)
   It/you must have been cold outside.

3. **あの映画はよかったでしょう。**(↘)／(↗)
   You must have enjoyed that movie.

つかれた
でしょう。

In the following examples, the speaker is asking the listener to confirm his assumption(④):

4. **あの人は山田さんだろう。**(↗) *That man must be Yamada-san, right?*

5. **あしたでいいでしょう。**(↗) *Tomorrow will do, won't it?*

あの人は山田さん
だろう。

64

Ⅱ．〜だろうと思う: *I think that probably* 〜

Let's compare the following two sentences.

1. あしたは雨でしょう。　　　　*It'll probably rain tomorrow.*

2. あしたは雨だろうと思います。　*I think it'll probably rain tomorrow.*

GN

Both sentences express uncertainty, but **〜と思う** *I think* 〜 implies a personal opinion, so unlike the weatherman on TV who uses **雨でしょう** on the basis of information from the Met (meteorological) Office, you would say **雨だろうと思う** if you base your assumption on the odd dark cloud in the sky.

	Plain form	
[V]	見る、見た、見ない 見なかった、見ている 見ていない、……	だろう でしょう
[A]	赤い 赤かった 赤くない 赤くなかった	
[NA]	親切* 親切だった 親切じゃない 親切じゃなかった	
[N]	雨* 雨だった 雨じゃない 雨じゃなかった	

* Note that the non-past positive of [NA] and [N] are exceptional in that the form before だろう is not the plain form.

$$\text{親切だ} + \text{だろう} \quad → \quad \text{親切だろう}$$
$$\text{雨だ} + \text{だろう} \quad → \quad \text{雨だろう}$$

Ⅲ. 〜そうだ〈2〉: *I have heard that* 〜

Examples

① 田中さんは来月結婚するそうです。
I've heard that Tanaka-san will get married next month.

② この店はカメラが安いそうだ。
They say cameras are cheap at this shop.

③ ここは静かだそうだ。　　　　　　*I've heard it's quiet here.*

④ あの人は川田さんじゃないそうだ。 *I've heard that that man isn't Kawada-san.*

【*Explanation*】

Attached to the plain form, そうです／そうだ *I have heard (that)*〜, *They say (that)*〜 indicates that a statement is based on information from elsewhere.

Be careful not to confuse this with そうです *looks like* we had in Lesson 17.
⇨L17GNⅢ

Compare the pairs of sentences:

1. 午後は雨がふるそうです。
   (plain form ＋そうです)

   They say it's going to rain in the afternoon.

2. 午後は雨がふりそうです。
   ([V(base)]＋そうです)

   It looks like it's going to rain this afternoon.

3. この料理はおいしいそうです。
   (plain form ＋そうです)

   I understand that this dish is delicious.

66

4. この料理はおいしそうです。（[A(stem)]＋そうです）
   This dish looks delicious.

〜とのことです is often used in place of 〜そうです for conveying messages in a business-like manner, like a secretary informing the company president:

5. そのことでお返事がほしいとのことです。
   They said that they want an answer on that.

GN

Ⅳ. 〜つもりだ: *intend to* 〜

〜つもりだ is used to express your intention:

1. 夏休みにアンケート調査をするつもりです。
   I intend to conduct a questionnaire survey during the summer vacation.

2. 国へは帰らないつもりです。
   I don't intend to return to my home country.

3. この荷物をほんとうに全部持っていくつもりですか。
   Do you really mean to take all this luggage with you?

　〜つもりだ, attached to plain non-past verbs, expresses the speaker's intention. In a question（〜つもりか／〜つもりですか）, it is used to ask about other people's intentions. As 〜つもりだ is concerned with intentions, it is attached to controllable verbs.

Ⅴ. *Keego*「敬語」〈4〉: *passive honorifics*

Examples

① 木村先生は帰られました。　　　　*Kimura-sensee has gone home.*

② A：いつ日本に来られましたか。　*When did you come to Japan?*

　 B：先月まいりました。　　　　　*I came last month.*

【*Explanation*】

We saw that Japanese uses two types of honorific verbs, regular and irregular. Another type of regular honorific verb is the passive honorific, in which the passive form of most verbs can be used as an honorific verb; these verbs no longer have a passive meaning: ⇨L9GNVI, 10GNVII, 17GNIV

木村先生はお帰りになりました。　*Kimura-sensee has already gone home.*
↓
木村先生は帰られました。

いつ日本にいらっしゃいましたか。　*When did you come to Japan?*
↓
いつ日本に来られましたか。

木村先生がお話しになります。　*Kimura-sensee will give a talk.*
↓
木村先生が話されます。

Can you tell the difference between the pairs?

1. a　先生は学生をほめられました。　*The teacher praised the student.*

   b　学生は先生にほめられました。　*The student was praised by the teacher.*

2. a　先生がそう言われました。　*The teacher said so.*

   b　先生にそう言われました。　*(I) was told so by the teacher.*

3. a　山田さんが注意されました。　*Yamada-san cautioned (someone).*

   b　山田さんに注意されました。　*(I) was cautioned by Yamada-san.*

The passive honorific sounds somewhat informal and is popular among young people.

Passive honorifics		
Ordinary　verbs	Non-past pos.	Non-past neg.

	Ordinary verbs		Non-past pos.	Non-past neg.
Group Ⅰ -u ↓ -areru	hanasu 話す	*to talk*	hanasareru 話される	hanasarenai 話されない
	nomu 飲む	*to drink*	nomareru 飲まれる	nomarenai 飲まれない
	au 会う	*to meet*	awareru 会われる	awarenai 会われない
	isogu 急ぐ	*to hurry*	isogareru 急がれる	isogarenai 急がれない
Group Ⅱ -ru ↓ -rareru	oriru 降りる	*to get off*	orirareru 降りられる	orirarenai 降りられない
	kariru 借りる	*to borrow*	karirareru 借りられる	karirarenai 借りられない
	akeru 開ける	*to open*	akerareru 開けられる	akerarenai 開けられない
Group Ⅲ	kuru 来る	*to come*	korareru 来られる	korarenai 来られない
	suru する	*to do*	sareru される	sarenai されない

1. A：お酒は飲まれますか。　*Do you drink sake?*

   B：ええ、いただきます。　*Yes, I do.*

2. A：急がれますか。　*Are you in a hurry?*

   B：いいえ、急ぎませんが。　*No, I'm not.*

3. A：どこで降りられますか。　*Where will you get off?*

   B：次で降りるんですが。　*I'll get off at the next station.*

4. A：結婚されていますか。　*Are you married?*

   B：ええ、去年結婚しました。　*Yes, I got married last year.*

GN

Ⅵ. 〜ながら: (doing something) *while* (doing something else)

Examples

① コーヒーを飲みながら、手紙を書いた。
I wrote a letter while drinking coffee.

② アルバイトをしながら、大学で勉強した。
I went to university while doing a part-time job.

【*Explanation*】

{S₁} ながら、 {S₂} is used when the same person does two different actions at the same time; {S₁} and {S₂} can either occur simultaneously (①), or during the same extended period of time (②).

> {S₁[V(base)]} ながら、{S₂}
> コーヒーを飲みながら、手紙を書いた。

{S₂} indicates the more important or main action; see how ① changes if the order is reversed and コーヒーを飲む becomes the main action:

手紙を書きながら、コーヒーを飲んだ。
I drank coffee while writing a letter.

Ⅶ. The こ/そ/あ/ど system〈2〉: こんな・そんな・あんな・どんな〜 ...*sort of* 〜

GN

Examples

① A：どんなセーターが好きですか。
　　What kind of sweater do you like?

　B：赤いセーターが好きです。
　　I like red sweaters.

　　こんなセーターが好きです。
　　I like sweaters like this one.

② こんな家に住みたい。
　I want to live in a house like this.

③ あんな人はきらいです。
　I hate that sort of man.

④ そんなに大きい荷物を持って
　どこへ行くんですか。
　Where are you going with
　such a big package?

【*Explanation*】

　　こんな・そんな・あんな are used before nouns to describe them in the sense of *a* [N] *like this/that, this/that sort of* [N]. The choice between こ／そ／あ is the same as for other members of the こ／そ／あ series. ⇨L4GNI For questions (*what kind of* [N]), どんな [N] is used. ⇨L10GNI

　　To indicate extent (*this〜/that〜*) with verbs or adjectives, こんなに／そんなに／あんなに is used:

1. そんなに高くありません。
   It is not (all) that expensive.

2. あんなにたくさん人がいる。
   Look how many people there are!
   (lit. There are so many people.)

3. こんなに買いました。
   Look how much I bought!
   (lit. I bought this much.)

VIII. ～でも: ~ or something

Examples

① お茶でも飲みましょう。
   Let's drink tea or something.

② あしたは一日中ひまだし、東京へでも行こうかな。
   Tomorrow I am free all day, so I might go to Tokyo or somewhere.

【*Explanation*】

Adding **でも** to a noun makes a statement, suggestion or question less direct or committed. In ①, there is no commitment to **お茶** (**コーヒー** or **ビール** will do just as well); the suggestion is having a cup or glass of something, e.g. tea. Likewise, in ② the speaker is not necessarily committed to going to **東京**.

Before **でも**, **が** and **を** are dropped, whereas other particles like **に、へ、で、と、まで、から、** precede **でも** as follows: ⇨L3GNⅦ

1. 頭が痛いんですか。 → 頭でも痛いんですか。
   Do you have a headache (or some other problem)?

2. お茶を飲みましょう。 → お茶でも飲みましょう。
   Let's have some tea or something.

3. 東京へ行きたい。 → 東京へでも行きたい。
   I want to go to Tokyo or somewhere.

72

Conversation Notes

<General Information>

1. The Japanese house

Below you see an advertisement for selling a house—for ¥50,000,000. Buying such a house is only a dream for the average Japanese "salaryman"; land prices in Japan, especially near Tokyo, make owning a house beyond his reach.

Let's look at the floor plan of a Japanese house:

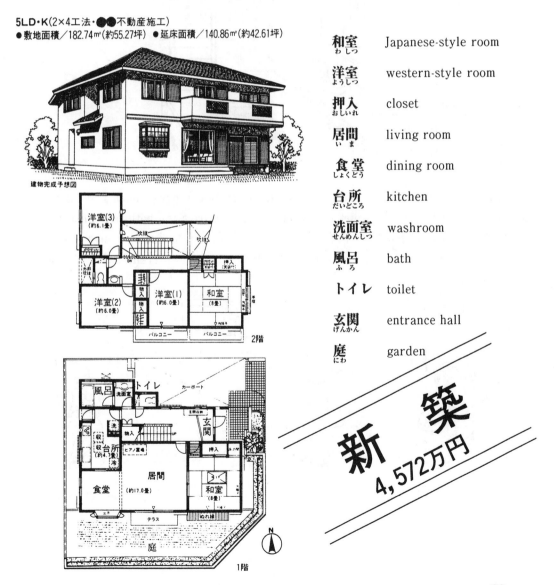

和室	Japanese-style room
わ しつ	
洋室	western-style room
ようしつ	
押入	closet
おしいれ	
居間	living room
い ま	
食堂	dining room
しょくどう	
台所	kitchen
だいどころ	
洗面室	washroom
せんめんしつ	
風呂	bath
ふ ろ	
トイレ	toilet
玄関	entrance hall
げんかん	
庭	garden
にわ	

Traditionally, the Japanese house was built of wood, but nowadays concrete structures with a Western appearance are also used. Most of the interior, however, remains Japanese style: most rooms are interconnected by **ふすま** (sliding doors) and floors are covered with **たたみ** (thick rice-straw mats); people do not wear shoes inside the house.

In most cases, Japanese-style rooms have closets called **押入**. The alcove (called **床の間**) is located in the room used for entertaining visitors. A hanging scroll (calligraphy or a painting) is displayed on the wall of the **床の間**, and a flower arrangement called **生け花** is placed under the scroll. **しょうじ** are paper-covered sliding screens:

しょうじ

たたみ

床の間
Alcove

Japanese-style toilets require the user to squat, but in newer homes, Western-style toilets are often found. The toilet is normally separate from the bathroom; to ask to use it, **「すみません、お手洗い（トイレ）をお借りしたいんですが。」** can be used. Note the difference in the direction the user faces when using the different styles of toilet:

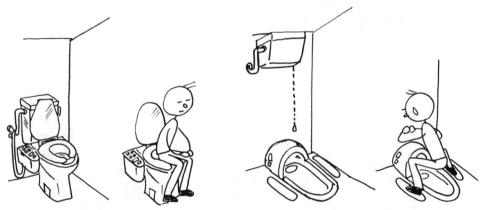

Western-style toilet

Japanese-style toilet

2. Bowing

Bowing or nodding accompanies most greetings in Japan, from introductions to meeting acquaintances. Bowing comes in a variety of degrees and duration, depending on the formality of the occasion; a receptionist in a company or at a department store, for instance, will bow slowly and deeply, whereas a short, light bow is appropriate for a visit to the home of a friend. Depending on the situation, expressions like **こんにちは** or **はじめまして** are said while bowing.

In a Japanese-style room, bows are executed in a different way in that you kneel on the **たたみ** or **ざぶとん** (*a Japanese cushion*) and lower your upper torso until it is almost parallel with the floor, supporting yourself with your hands on the **たたみ**. Look at the illustrations:

3. Giving a present

When you visit someone's home, it is usual to take a present, e.g. souvenir from your country, or sweets. It is not necessary to take an expensive gift every time you visit someone's house, but the Japanese appreciate little presents, such as something from your home town.

In Lesson 13, we saw verbs of giving like **あげる** and **さしあげる**, the latter being a superpolite variant of **あげる**.

The below are, however, not appropriate for gift-giving.

（×）　学生：先生にこれをさしあげます。

（×）　学生：先生、これをさしあげたいんですが。

To offer a gift in a formal situation, 「**つまらないものですが、どうぞ。**」is most commonly used. **つまらないもの** is an expression of understatement (*lit. something insignificant/worthless*), used, of course, with quite valuable presents, too! Some similar expressions are:

① **ほんのすこしですが、どうぞ。**
　　It's nothing much, but please (accept it).

② **ほんの気持ちですから、どうぞ。**
It's a token of my gratitude, so please accept it.

When giving a gift, 「**ほんの気持ちです。**」 is often used (**ほんの** *merely, only* expresses modesty). Nowadays, younger Japanese often prefer to use more direct expressions:

① **これ国のおみやげです。どうぞ。**
This is a present from my country. Please accept it.

② **チョコレートです。みなさんでどうぞ。**
Here's some chocolate. Please enjoy it.

Some Japanese will hesitate before accepting a present, as an expression of modesty.

A：これ国のおみやげです。どうぞ。
B：いや。そんなに心配しないでください。
A：でも、ほんの気持ちですから。
B：そうですか。じゃ、どうも。

4. Meals

When offering food or drink, your host will often say 「**えんりょなくめしあがってください。**」 or 「**ごえんりょなく。**」 *Please feel free to eat a lot.* ⇨MC., N.W. **えんりょ** (*reserve/hesitation*) is applied to show the expected degree of modesty in front of people who are superiors or relative strangers; it complements the use of ***Keego***.

If for religious or other reasons you do not eat certain foods, you can inform your host as follows:

A：すみません。豚肉は｜食べられないんです。
　　　　　　　　　｜**だめなんです。**
I'm sorry but I can't eat pork.

B：そうですか。じゃ、ほかのものをお持ちしましょう。
I see. In that case, I will serve some other things.

You can use the same expressions to make your host aware in case you find yourself growing tired of Japanese cuisine, preferably beforehand.

Before and after the meal, the following expressions can be used.

Wow! That looks delicious. Thank you.
We have nothing much, but...

Thank you for a wonderful meal.
Not. at all.

5. The Japanese bath

The bathroom in a Japanese home is designed for cleaning one's body before one soaks in the tub; this is done while sitting on a stool on the tiled area OUTSIDE the tub, so the water in the tub remains clean and can be used for several family members in turn. (Bathing practices do vary, however, from home to home.) Remember to leave the water in the bath tub after you finish your bath, and never use soap inside the tub.

1. Rinse your body with water from the tub.

2. Get in the tub.

3. Wash outside of the tub.

4. Return to the tub to soak.

<Strategies>

S-1. How to start a conversation —7. Visiting

When you visit the home of a friend or your professor, certain fixed expressions are used:

a. 玄関で *At the entrance hall*

    A：ごめんください。
       こんにちは。
       こんばんは。

    B：はい。どなたですか。

    A：山下です。

ごめんください *Excuse me* is used to attract attention at the entrance hall, a bit like English *Hello*. Most houses now use doorbells, interphones, etc. which sometimes make it unnecessary to say **ごめんください**. In that case, the exchange of greetings may be like this:

    A：（Sound of chime）
    B：いらっしゃい。😊
       よく、いらっしゃいました。📺
      Welcome/Thank you for coming.

    どうぞ、｜お上がりください。📺
         ｜お入りください。
    Please, come in.

    A：｜失礼します。📺
      ｜おじゃまします。
    Thank you.

「どうぞ、お上がりください。」 is used when asking someone to step up into a Japanese-style house, whereas **お入りください** is used when asking someone to enter a room or a Western-style house.

When entering someone's home or starting to talk, **おじゃまします** *lit. Excuse the disturbance* is used, whereas **おじゃましました** is used when one has finished talking and leaves.

Similar expressions are **失礼します** and **失礼しました**. **失礼** literally means *being rude* and can be used to refer to various actions, for example, entering as well as leaving a room.

b. 部屋で　*In the room*

A：どうぞ、｜おすわりください。　*Please have a seat.*
　　　　　　　おかけください。

B：失礼します。　*Thank you.*

A：お楽にしてください。　*Please make yourself comfortable.*

In a Western-style room, your host or hostess will ask you to take a seat on a chair, whereas in a Japanese-style room you're asked to sit on a **ざぶとん**. Sitting Japanese style is tiring (and formal), so your host will invite you to sit in a less formal way, with your legs crossed. **どうぞ、お楽にしてください** means *Please make yourself comfortable.*

正座（せいざ）
formal sitting

あぐら
for men

足をくずす（あし）
for women

S-2. How to express praise

Praising, and expressing modesty when praised, is a social convention that is given much importance in Japan. The following expressions come in handy:

a.

あら、
かわいい
おじょうさん
だこと。

いいえ、
とんでも
ない。

Oh, how cute your daughter is!

Oh no. Not in the slightest.

b.

まあ、
すごい
コート!
高かった
でしょ?

いいえ、
ほんの
安ものよ
ホホホ

Wow, what a gorgeous coat!
It must have been be expensive?
No, no. It was quite cheap.

c.

いえ、
それほどでも…。

ほう。えが
お上手ですね。

Gee, you are good at painting.
No, not really.

d.

いいお部屋
ですね。

いいえ、
とんでもないです。

It's a nice room.
No, not at all.

80

S-3.　How to end a conversation —4. Visiting

a. When you want to take your leave, you can use the following:

①A：じゃ、そろそろ。（失礼します。）
I must get going.

B：まだいいじゃありませんか。
It's still early. Stay for a while.

もうそろそろ signals that you wish to end the conversation and leave. The hostess or host will usually reply「**まだ、いいじゃないですか。**」or「**もうちょっといいでしょう。**」. If you have a particular reason why you need to leave, you can give it.

②A：もうそろそろ。

B：まだいいじゃないですか。

A：ええ。でも、ゼミの準備がありますので。
Well, I have to prepare for tomorrow's seminar.

b. Thanking the host when leaving

When leaving, express your thanks to the host or hostess:

①A：きょうはほんとうにありがとうございました。
Thank you very much for your hospitality.

B：また来てくださいね。
Please come again.

②A：どうもごちそうさまでした。
Thank you very much for your meal.

B：いいえ、何のおかまいもしませんで。
I'm sorry that we couldn't take better care of you.

A：いいえ、とても楽しかったです。
I've had a wonderful time.

「**どうもごちそうさまでした。**」expresses thanks for food and drink.「**何のおかまいもしませんで。**」is a conventional response to「**ごちそうさまでした。**」.

c. Thanking the host after the visit.

If you meet your host again after a few days, it is customary to thank him/her with expressions like 先日はどうも/この 間はどうも/etc.

A：先日は、どうもありがとうございました。とても楽しかったです。

Thank you very much for a wonderful time the other day. I had a great time.

B：いいえ。どういたしまして。また、来てくださいよ。

Not at all. Please come again.

If you have no chance to see him/her, you can send a thank-you letter, as in the report. ⇨Report

第20課

コピー機を使う
き　　つか
Using a photocopier

OBJECTIVES:

GRAMMAR

I . ～ことがある: *have (experienced ～)*
II . とき〈2〉: *at the time of, when*
III . ～ば: *if ～*
IV . ～かもしれない: *may ～/might ～*
V . ～すぎる: *too* (adjective)
VI . ～方: *how to ～*
　　　かた

CONVERSATION

＜General Information＞

1. Vocabulary used to explain a procedure: for a photocopier, cooking recipe, etc.

＜Strategies＞

S-1. How to start a conversation —8. Creating an opening
S-2. How to explain a procedure
S-3. How to ask for something to be done for you —2.
S-4. How to express an opinion

Model Conversation

Characters ：Yamashita(山下), Anil Sharma(アニル・シャルマ)

Situation ：Anil wants to make ten copies of class materials for Kimura-sensee's seminar. He asks Yamashita-san how to reduce the size from B4 to B5 in the seminar room.

Flow-chart ：

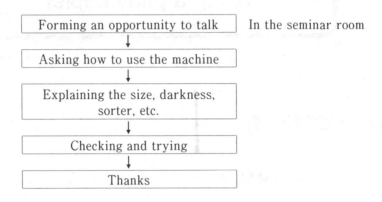

― 研究室で―

山　下　：アニルさん、何してんの。
シャルマ：ゼミの資料、コピーしたいんだけど。
山　下　：うん。
シャルマ：このコピー機、使ったことある。
山　下　：うん。
シャルマ：これ、縮小コピーしたいんだけど、やり方教えてもらえないかな。
山　下　：いいよ。

　　　　　　＊　　　　　＊　　　　　＊

シャルマ：これ、B4からB5にしたいんだけど。
山　下　：あ、縮小コピーする時はね、このボタンを押すんだ。
シャルマ：あ、これね。
山　下　：うん。B4からB5だから、ここに合わせて。
シャルマ：うん。(Pushing the button "B4→B5")
山　下　：用紙のサイズはB5にして。
シャルマ：ええと、B5ね。(Pushing the button for size "B5")
山　下　：うん。ちょっと1枚だけ、やってみて。

シャルマ：うん。(Setting a sheet of paper and pushing the start button)
山　下　：どう。
シャルマ：うん。縮小はできたけど、これ、ちょっとこすぎるかな。
山　下　：どれどれ。(Looking at the copy)
　　　　　ううん、そうだなあ。じゃ、これで調節して、(Pushing the "darker" button)
　　　　　もう一度やってみて。
シャルマ：うん。(Pushing the start button again)
山　下　：(Looking at the copy) あ、今度はちょうどいいんじゃない。
シャルマ：うん、そうだね。

　　　　　＊　　　＊　　　＊

山　下　：じゃあ、原稿を全部ここに置いて。
シャルマ：(Inserting the materials) ええと、10部いるから (Pushing "1" and "0")
山　下　：あ、ソーター、使ったほうがいいよ。
シャルマ：あ、そうか。このボタン。
山　下　：そう。「丁合い」のところ。
シャルマ：(Pushing the sorter button)
山　下　：あとは、スタートボタンを押せば、自動的に出てくるから。
シャルマ：うん。スタートボタンね。(Pushing the start button)

　　　　　＊　　　＊　　　＊

山　下　：うん、オーケー。これで、だいじょうぶ。
シャルマ：どうもありがとう。助かったよ。
山　下　：いやいや。

MC

Report

<コピー機の使い方>

　まず、コピー機の右側のところに原稿を下向きに置く。

　次に、数字のボタンを押してコピー枚数をセットする。10枚コピーする時は、「1」と「0」を押す。それから、用紙サイズに合わせて、トレイのボタンを押す。

　最後に、数字のボタンの右にある、一番大きなスタートボタンを押すと、左側の受け皿にコピーが出てくる。原稿は自動的に上に出る。

　コピー濃度を調節したい場合は、トレイボタンの右側のボタン、縮小コピーや拡大コピーをしたい場合は、トレイボタンの左側の矢印のボタンを押して合わせる。ソーターを使用する時は、一番左のボタンを「丁合い」に合わせる。

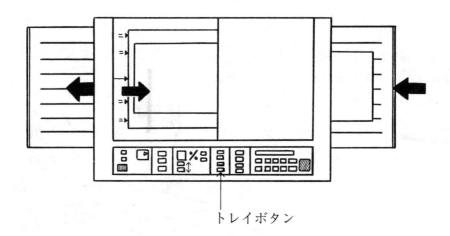

トレイボタン

New Words and Expressions

Words in the conversation

資料	しりょう	materials
縮小	しゅくしょう	reduction
やり方	やりかた	method, way, how to do
B4	ビーよん	B4 size（36×26cm）
B5	ビーご	B5 size（18×26cm）
ボタン		button
押す	おす	to push
合わせる	あわせる	to set
用紙	ようし	paper
こい		dark
調節する	ちょうせつする	to adjust
ちょうどいい		just right
原稿	げんこう	original
～部	～ぶ	～ copies
いる		to need
ソーター		sorter
丁合い	ちょうあい	sorter ＝ソーター
スタートボタン		start button
自動的に	じどうてきに	automatically
出てくる	でてくる	to come out, to appear
オーケー		O.K.

＜Expressions in the conversation＞

何してんの。↗   *What are you doing?*
なに
      Casual form of 何をしているんですか。 ⇨まとめ5BⅡ4
      ～んですか ⇨L13GNⅣ

使ったことある。↗   *Have you used it before?*
つか
      ＝使ったこと（が）ありますか。 ⇨GNⅠ

ここに合わせて。   *Set it here.*
あ

ちょっと1枚だけ、やってみて。   *Try making just one copy.*
まい

ちょっとこすぎるかな。↘   *Isn't it a little too dark, I wonder?*

　　　～すぎる ⇨GNV

どれどれ。   *Let me take a look.*

　　どれ alone also can be used for the same meaning. Notice that it is different
　　from どれ *which one?* here.

今度はちょうどいいんじゃない。↗   *This time it's just right, isn't it.* ⇨CN S-4
こんど

これで、だいじょうぶ。   *It's all right now.*

助かったよ。   *You've been a great help.*
たす

いやいや。   *Not at all.*

Words in the report

まず		*First*
下向きに置く	したむきにおく	*to place (it) face down*
次に	つぎに	*Next*
数字	すうじ	*numbers*
枚数	まいすう	*number of copies*
セットする		*to set*
トレイ		*paper tray*
最後に	さいごに	*Lastly*
受け皿	うけざら	*holding tray*
濃度	のうど	*darkness*
～場合	～ばあい	*in case ～, when ～*
拡大	かくだい	*enlargement*
矢印	やじるし	*arrow (sign)*
使用する	しようする	*to use* ＝使う

Grammar Notes

I. 〜ことがある: *have (experienced)* 〜

Examples

① A：富士山を見たことがありますか。
   Have you ever seen Mt. Fuji?

   B：いいえ、見たことがありません。
   No, I haven't.

② A：さしみを食べたことがありますか。
   Have you had sashimi before?

   B：ええ、一度食べたことがあります。
   Yes, I've had it once.

③ リサさんはさしみを食べたことがあるそうです。
   I understand that Lisa-san has eaten sashimi before.

④ そんな話は聞いたことがない。
   I've never heard such a story!

【*Explanation*】

To indicate that someone has performed or experienced an action before, use:

[V-ta] ことがある	------ *has (experienced)*（①②③）

食べたことがある。　　　　　*I've had it (once, twice...).*

[V-ta] ことがない	------ *has not experienced*（①④）

聞いたことがない。　　　*I've never heard of it.*

To show how often you have experienced something, use 一度／一回 *once*（②）, 二度／二回 *twice*, 三度／三回 *three times*, etc. To express that you have experienced something too often to count, use 何度も or 何回も *many times, often,* 一度も～ない／一回も～ない can be used to emphasize that you've never experienced something:

一度も聞いたことがない。　　*I've NEVER heard of it.*

Note that ～たことがある／ない concerns the presence or absence of an experience, whereas a particular action in the past is expressed with the past tense; compare the following examples:

1. A：○ もう昼ご飯を食べましたか。
   Have you eaten (today's) lunch yet?

   × 昼ご飯を食べたことがありますか。
   Have you ever eaten lunch (in your life)?

   B：○ ええ、食べました。
   Yes, I have.

   × ええ、食べたことがあります。
   Yes, I have (had lunch before).

2. A：10チャンネルの10時のニュースを見ましたか。
   Did you watch the 10 o'clock news on Channel 10 (last night)?

   B：ええ、見ました。おもしろかったですね。
   Yes, I did. It was interesting, wasn't it?

3. A：10チャンネルの10時のニュースを見たことがありますか。
   Have you ever watched the 10 o'clock news on Channel 10?

   B：ええ、見たことがありますよ。おもしろい番組ですね。
   Yes, I have watched it. It's an interesting program, isn't it?

4. A：きのう、木村先生に会いましたか。
   Did you meet Kimura-sensee yesterday?

   B：はい、会いました。
   Yes, I did.

5. A：木村先生に会ったことがありますか。
   Have you ever met Kimura-sensee?

   B：ええ、一度、会ったことがあります。
   Yes, I've met him once.

II. とき〈2〉: *at the time of, when*

Examples

① **母は手紙を読むとき、めがねをかける。**
  My mother puts on her glasses when she reads a letter.

② **晩ごはんを食べているとき、電話がなった。**
  While we were eating dinner, the telephone rang.

③ **私は国に帰ったとき、いつもカレーを買います。**
  I usually buy curry when I go back to my country.

④ **私は国に帰るとき、いつも日本のおみやげを買います。**
  I usually buy Japanese souvenirs when I go back to my country.

GN

【*Explanation*】

とき is similar to English *when* or *while* in *When I went to France, I bought a bag.* or *While I am in France, I will buy a bag.*

However, とき differs in some respects from English *when* or *while*; let's examine the following sentence to make these differences clear:

> {S₁}　　とき　　{S₂}
> **フランスへ行く　とき、　かばんを買う**　　　*I'll buy a bag when I go to France.*

1. Tense in とき clauses

The tense of {S₁} in Japanese indicates whether the action of {S₁} is completed or not at the time the action of {S₂} took place:

> [V-(r)u] とき　　　　→　uncompleted
> **フランスへ行くとき**　→　*before arriving in France*
> [V-ta] とき　　　　　→　completed
> **フランスへ行ったとき**　→　*after arriving in France*

91

! The tense of the whole sentence is shown by the main sentence, $\{S_2\}$. Note that even if the verb of $\{S_1\}$ is in the past, the whole sentence can still be in the future, because $\{S_1\}$ merely indicates that the action of $\{S_1\}$ will have been completed at the time of the action of $\{S_2\}$. Compare the following examples:

1. フランスへ行くとき、かばんを買った。

When I went to France, I bought a bag. (before I got to France.)

　行くとき　→　The action (of going) hadn't been completed when the speaker bought the bag.

2. フランスへ行ったとき、かばんを買った。

When I went to France, I bought a bag. (after I got to France.)

　行ったとき　→　The action (of going) had been completed when the speaker bought the bag.

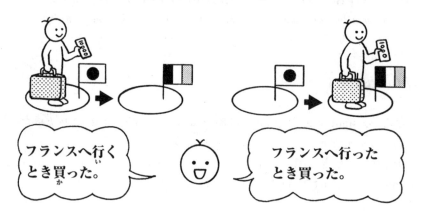

1. フランスへ行くとき、かばんを買う。

When I go to France, I'll buy a bag. (before I get to France.)

2. フランスへ行ったとき、かばんを買う。

When I go to France, I'll buy a bag. (after I get to France.)

The time relations between $\{S_1\}$ and $\{S_2\}$ are shown as above translation in ( ); unlike **[V-ta]** あとで *after* ~, **[V-te]** から *after* ~, and **[V-(r)u]** まえに *before* ~, ~とき essentially presents actions as being simultaneous. ⇨L12GNⅢ,Ⅳ,Ⅴ

2. Sentences using とき

When you make a sentence using **とき**, follow the combinations given in the table below.

~とき		
Plain form + **とき**		
[V]	読む 読まない 読んだ 読まなかった 読んでいる 読んでいない	*when one reads/read* *when one doesn't/didn't read* *when one reads/read* *when one doesn't/didn't read* *while one is/was reading* *while one isn't/wasn't reading or* *if one hasn't/hadn't read*
[A]	寒い 寒くない	*when it is/was cold* *when it isn't/wasn't cold*
[NA]	ひまな* ひまじゃない	*when one is/was free* *when one isn't/wasn't free*
[N]	子供の*	*when one was a child*

The middle column spanning all rows reads: **とき**

* Note that **とき** is attached to the plain form, except in the case of **[N]** だ and **[NA]** だ. ⇨L8GNⅨ

3. とき as a noun

とき is a noun meaning *time*, and therefore can be followed by particles like が, を, に, は, も:

1. 私はピアノをひいているときが一番楽しい。
   I am happiest when I'm playing the piano.
   (lit. The happiest time is when I'm playing the piano.)

2. A：毎晩、お酒を飲むんですか。
Do you drink every night?

B：いいえ、飲まないときもありますよ。
No, there are times when I don't.

The noun 〜場合, which means *occasion,* is also often used in the sense of *in case (of)* 〜*, if*:

1. わからない場合は事務室で聞いてください。
If/In case you don't understand, ask at the office.

2. 雨の場合は中止します。
In case of rain, we'll cancel.

III. 〜ば: *if*〜

Examples

① よく読めば、わかりますよ。
If you read it carefully, you'll understand it.

② いま行けば、間に合います。
If I leave now, I'll be on time.

③ 安ければ、買います。
If it's cheap, I'll buy it.

【*Explanation*】

1. {S₁} ば {S₂}

{S₁} ば indicates the conditions under which the action or state of {S₂} will become possible. As ば implies that {S₁} is still an unrealized event at the time the statement is made, it cannot be used with past tense forms (ば can be used with the past tense with a different meaning; we will deal with this at a later stage.)

There are also some idiomatic uses of 〜ば; the sentence ending 〜ばいい is used for giving/asking advice:

DRILLS:

Easier-to-follow English in the Instructions
Some changes to New Words in drills for some lessons
Changes in the SD, CD, T sections and etc.. as below.

CHANGES BETWEEN THE 1ST AND 2ND EDITIONS

In response to a great deal of very useful feedback from teachers and students using SFJ at home and abroad, we have decided to make some changes to the 2nd edition of this volume so as to make it better, easier-to-use product. Especially for institutions of learning where the 1st edition is still being used by some, it may be useful for the teacher to keep track of such changes, for which s/he is kindly referred to the information given below.

We invite all users of SFJ to contact us with further suggestions for improvement at address below.

Tsukuba Language Group
International Student Center
University of Tsukuba
1-1-1 Tennoudai, Tsukuba-shi 305
Japan

The authors

NOTES:

Easier-to-follow English in the explanations
A numbers of changes has been made as follows:

A：キャンセルするとき、どうすればいいですか。

What shall I do when I want to cancel?

B：電話をかければいいですよ。
でんわ

It's all right to phone.

2. Points to pay attention to when using と，ば，and たら

The use of と and たら overlaps somewhat with that of ば. There are cases in which all three can be used, and others where only one of them is possible, so it is useful to review the use of と, ば, and たら to establish differences:

1）と ⇨L12GN I

と most commonly indiates that the relationship between $\{S_1\}$ and $\{S_2\}$ is one of habitual consequence; と is therefore not used for particular or individual events, and sentence endings such as ～てください, ～たい, ～ましょう, ～ませんか, which express the speaker's intention, request, wishes or suggestion, are not used with と.

2）ば

ば is not normally used for expressing the speaker's intention, request, wishes or suggestions. Remember also that the past tense is not used in $\{S_1\}$ ば $\{S_2\}$ sentences.

3）たら ⇨L11GN I

たら can be used for particular and individual events and unexpected results; it is commonly be used in sentences which express the speaker's intention, request wishes, etc.

たら is often used in place of ば and と in conversation, but is avoided in reports and newspapers.

3. The ば form

The ば form is formed as shown in the following table. Note that the positive form of nouns and adjective use なら rather than ば.

— *ba form*			
	Dic. from	Positive	Negative
[V] Group Ⅰ	yomu　*to read* 読む	yomeba 読めば	yomanakereba 読まなければ
	osu　*to push* 押す	oseba 押せば	osanakereba 押さなければ
Group Ⅱ	miru　*to see* 見る	mireba 見れば	minakereba 見なければ
	ireru　*to put in* 入れる	irereba 入れれば	irenakereba 入れなければ
Group Ⅲ	suru　*to do* する	sureba すれば	shinakereba しなければ
	kuru　*to come* 来る	kureba 来れば	konakereba 来なければ
[A]	samui　*cold* 寒い	samukereba 寒ければ	samuku nakereba 寒くなければ
	yasui　*cheap* 安い	yasukereba 安ければ	yasuku nakereba 安くなければ
	ii　*good* いい	yokereba よければ	yoku nakereba よくなければ
[NA]	shizuka da　*quiet* 静かだ	shizuka nara 静かなら	shizuka ja nakereba 静かじゃなければ
[N]	gakusee da　*student* 学生だ	gakusee nara 学生なら	gakusee ja nakereba 学生じゃなければ

Ⅳ. ～かもしれない: *may ～ /might ～*

Examples

① あしたは雨(あめ)かもしれません。　*It may/might rain tomorrow.*

② 来月(らいげつ)はひまかもしれない。　*I may be free tomorrow.*

③ 秋葉原(あきはばら)のほうが安(やす)かったかもしれない。
It might have been cheaper in Akihabara.

④ 実験(じっけん)は成功(せいこう)するかもしれません。　*The experiment may/might succeed.*

GN

【*Explanation*】

かもしれない indicates uncertainty *may* ～ */might* ～. The probability indicated by **かもしれない** is small:

1. 試験(しけん)に合格(ごうかく)しないかもしれません。　*I may not pass the examination.*

When the speaker is more certain about the likelihood of something happening, the following are used:

2. 試験に合格すると思(おも)う。　⇨L11GNⅡ

3. 試験に合格するだろう。　⇨L19GNⅠ

To make sentences with **かもしれない**, follow the patterns in the table below.

<table>
<tr><th colspan="3">Plain form ＋ かもしれない</th></tr>
<tr><td>[V]</td><td>来(く)る、来(き)た、来(こ)ない
来(こ)なかった、来(き)ている
来(き)ていない、……</td><td rowspan="2">かもしれない</td></tr>
<tr><td>[A]</td><td>寒(さむ)い
寒かった
寒くない
寒くなかった</td></tr>
</table>

[NA]	親切* しんせつ 親切だった 親切じゃない 親切じゃなかった	
[N]	先生* せんせい 先生だった 先生じゃない 先生じゃなかった	かもしれない

    * Note that **かもしれない** is attached to the plain form, except for [N] **だ** and [NA] **だ** in which case **だ** is dropped and **かもしれない** attached directly.

V. 〜すぎる: *too* (adjective)

Examples

① **この料理はからすぎる。**
   りょうり
   This dish is too hot/spicy.

② **ここはうるさすぎる。**
   It's too noisy here.

③ **夕べ飲みすぎて，今朝は頭がいたい。**
   ゆう の   けさ   あたま
   I drank too much last evening, and have a headache this morning.

④ **遠くへ来すぎた。**
   とお   き
   I've come too far.

【*Explanation*】

    すぎる is added after [V], [A], or [NA] and implies that the action or state of the preceding word is excessive; the implication is usually negative.

    The word plus **すぎる** becomes a Group Ⅱ verb, conjugating **−すぎる, −すぎない, −すぎた, −すぎなかった**.

```
┌─────────────────────┐
│ [V(base)]           │         ┌─────────┐
│ [A] (without い)    │    +    │ すぎる  │
│ [NA] (without な)   │         └─────────┘
└─────────────────────┘
```

飲みすぎた　　*drank too much*
からすぎない　*not too hot/spicy*
うるさすぎる　*too noisy*
静かすぎる　　*too quiet*

┌────────────────────────────┐
│ **Ⅵ.　～方**: *how to ～* │
│ 　　かた   │
└────────────────────────────┘

GN

Examples
---

①　この料理の作り方を教えてください。
　　りょうり　つく　　おし
　Please show me how to make this dish.

②　このコンピュータの使い方がわからない。
　　　　　　　　　　　　つか
　I don't know how to use this computer.

【*Explanation*】

　　～方 is attached to the verb base, giving it the meaning of how to (do something), the way of (doing something). The combination [V(base)] ＋ 方 is a noun phrase, taking particles like が, を etc. Look at the following pairs of examples, paying attention to the particles.

　　1. お母さんが育てます。　　　　　*The mother raises (her children).*
　　　　かあ　　そだ
　　　　お母さんの育て方はいい。　　*The mother's way of raising (her children) is good.*

　　2. 料理を作ります。　　　　　　　*(Someone) makes the food.*
　　　　料理の作り方を教えてください。　*Please tell me how to make the food.*

　　3. ワープロを使います。　　　　　*(Someone) uses a word processor.*
　　　　ワープロの使い方がわからない。　*I don't know how to use the word processor.*

　　4. つくばへ／に行きます。　　　　*(Someone) goes to Tsukuba.*
　　　　つくばへの行き方が書いてある。　*It shows how to get to Tsukuba.*

　　Note how the particles, indicated by ▓ change: が→の, を→の, and へ→への. (にの is never used.)

Conversation Notes

<*General Information*>

1. Vocabulary used to explain a procedure

a. Operating instructions for photocopier:

1. スイッチ	*main switch*	
2. 電源 (でんげん)	*power*	
3. コントロールパネル	*control panel*	
4. コピー受け (う)	*copy tray*	
5. トレイ	*tray*	
6. 原稿 (げんこう)	*original*	
7. 用紙 (ようし)	*copy paper*	
8. 機能 (きのう)	*function*	
9. セットする	*to set*	
10. 選ぶ (えら)	*to select*	
11. 倍率 (ばいりつ)	*reproduction ratio*	
12. 任意 (にんい)	*zoom, option*	
13. 固定 (こてい)	*fixed*	
14. 縮小 (しゅくしょう)	*reduce*	
15. 拡大 (かくだい)	*enlarge*	
16. 等倍 (とうばい)	*full size*	
17. 濃度 (のうど)	*light/dark level*	
18. 自動 (じどう)	*auto (matic)*	
19. こく	*darker*	
20. うすく	*lighter*	
21. ソーター	*sorter* = 丁合い (ちょうあ)	

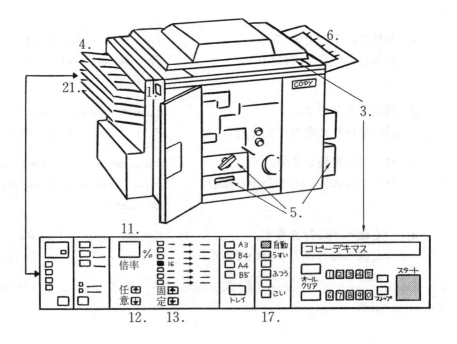

b. For recipes

（1）Tools

1.	なべ	*saucepan, pot*	12.	フォーク	*fork*
2.	フライパン	*frying pan*	13.	ナイフ	*knife*
3.	おたま	*ladle*	14.	ほうちょう	*kitchen knife*
4.	あわだてき	*whisk*	15.	まないた	*chopping board*
5.	やかん	*kettle*	16.	さら	*plate, dish*
6.	ガス台	*stove*	17.	茶わん	*cup, bowl*
7.	オーブン	*oven*	18.	おわん	*soup bowl* (wooden)
8.	電子レンジ	*microwave oven*	19.	コップ	*glass* (for water, milk, etc.)
9.	ボール	*bowl*			
10.	カップ	*measuring cup*			
11.	スプーン	*spoon*			

cf. 大さじ　*tablespoon*
cf. 小さじ　*teaspoon*

20. グラス　*glass* (for wine, champagne, etc.)

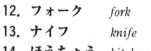

（2） Ingredients

牛肉	ぎゅうにく	beef
豚肉	ぶたにく	pork
鳥肉	とりにく	chicken
魚	さかな	fish
野菜	やさい	vegetables
卵／玉子	たまご	egg
チーズ		cheese
豆腐	とうふ	bean curd
小麦粉	こむぎこ	wheat flour
油	あぶら	oil, fat
バター		butter
調味料	ちょうみりょう	seasonings

しお	salt	さとう	sugar
こしょう	pepper	しょうゆ	soy sauce
す	vinegar	しょうが	ginger
にんにく	garlic	わさび	horse radish
からし	mustard	とうがらし	red pepper
みりん	sweet SAKE	みそ	bean paste
スープのもと	soup stock	だし	fish stock

（3） Verbs for cooking techniques

1. まぜる — to mix
2. 煮る — to cook in stock
3. ゆでる — to boil (without seasonings)
4. 蒸す — to steam
5. 焼く — to grill, to roast, to broil
6. 炒める — to (shallow) fry
7. 揚げる — to deep-fry
8. 味をつける — to season
9. ふっとうする — come to a boil
   ふっとうさせる — bring to a boil
10. とける — to melt
    とかす — to melt, to dissolve (something)

（4）Expressions for quantity

1杯	いっぱい	*a cup, a spoonful of*
2杯	にはい	*two cups, two spoonfuls of*
3杯	さんばい	*three cups, three spoonfuls of*
〜杯	〜ぱい／はい／ばい	*〜 cup(s), 〜 spoonful(s) of*
半分	はんぶん	*a half*
1/2	にぶんのいち	*a half*
1/3	さんぶんのいち	*a third*
1/4	よんぶんのいち	*a quarter*
1/5	ごぶんのいち	*a fifth*
2倍	にばい	*double, twice as much as*
3倍	さんばい	*treble, three times*
4倍	よんばい	*quadruple, four times*
5倍	ごばい	*quintuple, five times*

c. For making Origami

おもて		*surface, face*
うら		*reverse side, back side*
線	せん	*line*
点線	てんせん	*dotted line*
折る	おる	*to fold*
開く	ひらく	*to open*
反対にする	はんたいにする	*to turn upside down*
ひっくり返す	ひっくりかえす	*to turn over*

折る　　　　　　開く

反対にする　　　ひっくり返す

103

<Strategies>

S-1. How to start a conversation —8. Creating an opening

When you meet someone for the first time on that day, you can start a conversation with greetings like **おはよう** and **こんにちは**. ⇨L1CN S-1

In other cases, you need to create an opening. There are several ways of doing this:

a. When a person is doing something, you can show your interest by asking what s/he is doing. Note that kind of question can be asked only to juniors or equals.

① A：何（を）｜ してんの。↗／して（い）るの。↗ 🇨🇦➡⬇
なに ｜ して（い）るんですか。↗ 🇯🇵➡⬇

What are you doing?

B：ゼミの資料｜ コピーして（い）るんだ。🇨🇦
しりょう ｜ コピーして（い）るんです。🇯🇵

I'm copying some materials for the seminar.

If the person seems to be looking for something/someone or having trouble, you can ask like this:

② A：どう｜ したの。↗ 🇨🇦   *What's the matter?*
｜ したんですか。🇯🇵
｜ なさったんですか。🇯🇵⬆

B：ゼミの資料｜ コピーしたいんだけど。🇨🇦
｜ コピーしたいんですけど。🇯🇵

I want to copy materials for the seminar, but...

The last **けど** shows that the person is having some trouble: B-san wants to copy materials for the seminar but s/he doesn't know how to use the photocopier.

b. You can create an opening by praising the other person's clothes or belongings: ⇨L19CN S-2

①🇨🇦Two men are talking:
A：お、いいネクタイしてるね。   *Oh, you are wearing a nice tie.*

B：そうかな。
Do you think so?

A：どこで買ったんだい。↗
Where did you get it?

B：ジャスコ。千円だったよ。
JUSCO. It cost 1,000 yen.

A：ふうん。↗　いいなあ。ところで、……
Really. That's not bad. By the way, ... (continued)

② 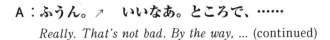Two women are talking:

A：あら、すてきなぼうしですね。
Oh, what a pretty hat.

B：いえ、いえ、そんなことないですよ。
No, no, not at all.

A：色がとてもすてきですわ。
Really nice colour.

B：そうかしら。どうも。実は、これ、パリで買ったんです。
Really? Thank you. In fact, I bought this in Paris.

A：そうですか。ああ、パリといえば、……
I see. Oh, speaking of Paris, ... (continued)

c. The Japanese often start a conversation by talking about the weather:

① 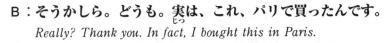A：また雨ですね。　　　　　　*It's raining again.*

B：そうですね。　　　　　　　*It is, isn't it.*

A：今年はよく降りますね。　*It's raining a lot this year.*

B：ええ。　　　　　　　　　　*Yes.*

A：台風が来て(い)るらしいですよ。
I heard that a typhoon is coming.

B：そうですか。そうそう、台風っていえば、……
Really? Oh yes, speaking of typhoons, ... (continued)

CN

② © A：あついね。
Hot, isn't it.

B：うん。こうあついと、なんにもできなくて。
Yes. In this sort of heat, one can't do anything.

A：おたく、エアコンは。↗
Do you have an air-conditioner?

B：実はね、……
In fact, ... (continued)

S-2. How to explain a procedure

a. To explain a procedure, for example, how to make something or use something, you can use expressions indicating the order of actions, such as まず／はじめに *first, firstly*, 次に *next, secondly*, それから *after that, then*, そして *and*, 最後に *at last, lastly*:

① まず、原稿カバーを開けて、原稿をおいて、閉めます。
First, open the cover, place the original (on the machine) and close it.

② 次に、コピー枚数をセットします。
Next, set the number of copies.

③ それから、用紙のサイズを選びます。
Then, choose the paper size.

④ 最後に、スタートボタンを押すと、受け皿にコピーが出てきます。
Last, when you push the start button, the copy will come out on the copy tray.

①  ②  ③ 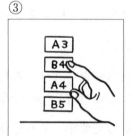 ④

b. To cover optional aspects of the procedure, use expressions like 〜場合は in case 〜, 〜時は when 〜:

① 拡大したい場合は、その倍率を選択してください。
In case you want to enlarge, choose the ratio.

② ソーターを使用する時は、ボタンを「丁合い」に合わせます。
When you use the sorter, set the button to "SORTER".

c. To explain successive actions, 〜て *and* and 〜てから *after* are used. To finish, 〜とできあがり *do 〜 and it'll be ready* or 〜(れ)ばいい *all you need to do is to do 〜* can be used:

① 三 A：ここに原稿を置いて、 *Place the original here.*

B：はい。 *Yes.*

A：コピー枚数をセットして、 *Set the number of copies.*

B：はい。 *I see.*

A：用紙のサイズを選んで、 *Select the paper size.*

B：はい。 *Right.*

A：スタート・ボタンを押せば、いいんです。 *Then all you need to do is to push the start button.*

② C A：水に材料を入れて、 *Put the ingredients in water.*

B：うん。 *Aha.*

A：ふっとうしてから、20分ぐらい煮て、 *Bring to the boil and cook for 20 minutes.*

B：それから。↗ *And then?*

A：調味料を入れるとできあがり。 *Add seasoning, and it'll be ready.*

While listening to explanations as the above, the listener will use *Aizuchi* such as うん, ええ, はい, そう↘, ふうん↗, なるほど, and so on. ⇨まとめ2BⅡ3, まとめ3BⅡ2

S-3. How to ask for something to be done for you —2.

a. To ask something of a friend in a casual way, you can ask directly as follows:
⇨L14GN I，II

～んだけど、	～てもらえる（かな）。
	～てもらえない（かな）。
	～てくれる（かな）。
	～てくれない（かな）。

I want to do (something); *Can you do it for me?*

①これ、縮小コピーしたいんだけど、やり方教えてもらえないかな。↘
　　I want to make a reduced copy of this; can you tell me how to do it?

②ちょっと暑いんだけど、窓を開けてくれない。↗
　　I'm a little hot; can you open the window?

Recall that formal ways of asking for something were dealt with earlier.
⇨L11CN S-1

b. You can introduce your request with a preliminary question:

③A：折り紙って、知ってる。↗
　　Do you know Origami?

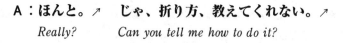

B：うん。つるなら、折れるけど。
　　Yes. I can make a crane.

A：ほんと。↗　　じゃ、折り方、教えてくれない。↗
　　Really?　　*Can you tell me how to do it?*

④A：このコピー機、使ったことある。↗
　　Have you used this copier before?

B：うん。
　　Yeah.

A：じゃ、ちょっと教えてもらいたいんだけど。
　　Can you tell me how to use it, then?

⑤📺A：タイのスープ、飲んだことありますか。
　　　Have you ever eaten Thai soup?

　　B：ええ。からいけど、おいしいですよね。
　　　Yes. It's hot but delicious, isn't it.

　　A：あの、もし作り方、ご存じなら、教えてくださいませんか。
　　　If you know how to make it, can you tell me, please.

S-4. How to express an opinion

CN

When asked your opinion on something, you can express it with 〜んじゃないで
しょうか, 〜んじゃない↗, etc.

　　A：これ、〜 ┃ でしょうか。📺
　　　　　　　　┃ かな／かしら。🐯
　　Do you think this is 〜?

　　B：┃ そうですね。〜んじゃないでしょうか。↘ 📺
　　　　┃ そうね。　　　〜んじゃない。↗ 🐯
　　Let me see.　　I think it's 〜.

Note that 〜んじゃない with rising intonation is not used as a negative, but is
similar in meaning to 〜と思う *I think 〜*.

①🐯A：これ、こすぎるかな。↘
　　　Do you think this is too dark?

　　B：そうね。いいんじゃない。↗
　　　Hmm..., I think it's OK.

②📺A：これ、ちょっとからすぎるでしょうか。↘
　　　Do you think this is too hot?

　　B：そうね。いいんじゃないでしょうか。↘
　　　Let's see; I think it's O.K.

Attached to a statement of facts, 〜んじゃない is used to ask for confirmation,
like English *isn't it, etc.* ⇨L17CN I　Compare the following:

③ⒼA：あした、テストがあるんじゃない。↗

You're having a test tomorrow, aren't you?

B：ああ、そうだったね。♟

Oh, yes, that's right.

④ⒺA：この問題、どうしたらいいでしょうか。↘
　　　　もんだい

What should I do about this problem?

B：ううん。↘　やめたほうがいいんじゃないでしょうか。↘

Hmm..., Hadn't you better give up?

まとめ　5

A. Grammar

Ⅰ. Summary of -i adjectives and na adjectives

1. -i adjectives inflect as follows.

> 1. [A-i]　（です）
> 2. [A-i] ＋ [N]
> 3. [A-ku] ＋ [V]

1) （1）このかばんは<u>大きい</u>です。　　　　*This bag is big.*

　　（2）これは<u>大きい</u>かばんです。　　　　*This is a big bag.*

　　（3）口を<u>大きく</u>あけてください。　　　*Open your mouth wide.*

2) （1）この店は<u>安い</u>です。　　　　　　*This shop is cheap.*

　　（2）この店には<u>安い</u>ものが置いてあります。
　　　　There are cheap goods in this shop.

　　（3）もっと<u>安く</u>してくださいませんか。
　　　　Could you make it any cheaper?

　　　　秋葉原に行くと、電気製品が<u>安く</u>買える。
　　　　If you go to Akihabara, you can buy electrical appliances cheaply.

Some more examples of **-i** adjectives used as adverbs:

　　　　早い　→　もっと<u>早く</u>来てください。
　　　　　　　　　Please come earlier.

　　　　遅い　→　山下さんはいつも<u>遅く</u>帰ってきます。
　　　　　　　　　Yamashita-san always comes home late.

　　　　小さい　→　テレビがうるさいので、もう少し音を<u>小さく</u>してください。
　　　　　　　　　The TV is too loud, so can you please turn down the volume a little.

痛い   →   食べすぎて、おなかが<u>痛く</u>なった。
I've eaten too much and now I have a stomach-ache.

ほしい → デパートに行くと、何でもすぐ<u>ほしく</u>なります。
When I go to a department store, I want everything.

食べたい→   ときどき国の料理が<u>食べたく</u>なります。
I sometimes feel like eating food from home.

2. na adjectives inflect as follows.

```
1. [NA] だ／です
2. [NA] な [N]
3. [NA] に [V]
```

1）1. アニルさんのアパートは<u>きれいです</u>。
Anil-san's apartment is clean/pretty.

   2. アニルさんは<u>きれいな</u>アパートに住んでいます。
Anil-san lives in a clean/pretty apartmemt.

   3. きのうそうじをしたら、部屋が<u>きれいに</u>なりました。
I cleaned the room yesterday, and it became nice and clean.

2）1. アニルさんは日本語が<u>上手</u>です。
Anil-san is good at Japanese.

   2. だれか日本語が<u>上手な</u>人はいませんか。
Is there anyone who speaks good Japanese?

   3. アニルさんは<u>上手に</u>日本語を話します。
Anil-san speaks Japanese well.

More examples of [**NA**] used as an adverb:

   4. うるさいから、<u>静かに</u>してください。
You are too noisy. Be quiet, please.

5. 地下鉄ができて、交通が便利になった。
   Since the underground/subway was built, transport has become convenient.

6. 病気がなおって、いまは元気に大学に行っています。
   I recovered from my illness, and am now going to the university cheerfully.

7. 事務室の人は、わからないことは何でも親切に教えてくれます。
   The people in the office kindly explain to us anything we don't understand.

8. 漢字はもっとていねいに書いてください。
   Write your Kanji more carefully.

9. はじめはきらいだったけど、だんだん好きになりました。
   At first I hated it, but gradually I got to like it.

Ⅱ. Verbs with many meanings

The following verbs have several meanings.

1. できる

1) *can*

1. 日本語を話すことができます。
   I can speak Japanese.

2. 図書館で本を借りることができますか。
   Can I borrow books from the library?

3. A：試験はできましたか。
   Did you do well in the exam?

   B：いえ、あまりできませんでした。
   No, not too well.

2） *to be ready/be completed*

1. ごはんができましたよ。
The meal's ready.

2. 写真はいつできますか。
When will the photos be ready?

3. 宿題がまだできていません。
I haven't finished my homework yet.

3） *to be built/come into being*

九州に新しい大学ができるそうです。
They say they're building a new university in Kyushu.

4） *to produce/grow*

私の国では一年中くだものができます。
In my country fruits grow all year round.

5） *to be made of*

この車のエンジンはセラミックスでできている。
The engine of this car is made from ceramics.

2. かける

1） *to telephone*　友だちに電話をかける。
I will telephone my friend.

2） *to lock*　かぎをかけるのを忘れました。
I forgot to lock (the door).

3） *to iron*　このシャツはアイロンをかけなくてもいい。
You need not iron this shirt.

4） *to hang, put on*　アニルさんは服を脱いでハンガーにかけた。
Anil-san took off his clothes and put them on a coat hanger.

5） *to sit*　どうぞここにおかけください。
Sit down here, please.

6） *to have (glasses) on*　テレビを見るときだけ、めがねをかけます。
I wear glasses only when I watch TV.

まとめ

7) *to multiply*　　１２３に３２１をかけると、いくらになるかな。
How much is 123 times 321?

8) *to sprinkle/pour on (spices)*

ごはんに塩（こしょう／さとう）をかけて食べる。
I eat rice sprinkled with salt (pepper/sugar).

9) *to cover with*　　寒いので、毛布をかけて寝ます。
It's cold, so I sleep with a blanket on.

10) *to cause worry*　　ご心配をかけて、すみませんでした。
I'm sorry to have worried you.

3.　とる

1) *to take*　　1.　自由にとってめしあがってください。
Help yourself. (lit., Take and eat freely.)

2.　すみませんが、そこの塩をとってくださいませんか。
Excuse me, could you pass me the salt (over there)?

3.　宿題を忘れたので、うちにとりに行ってきます。
I forgot to bring my home work, so I'll go home and get it.

2) *to steal*　　どろぼうにお金を20万円とられました。
I had 200,000 yen stolen by a burgler.

3) *to take off*　　寝るときには、めがねをとります。
When I go to sleep, I take off my glasses.

4) *to get old*　　年をとったら、一人で世界旅行に出かけようと思っている。
When I get old, I'd like to travel around the world by myself.

5) *to take a note*　　忘れないように、メモをとる。
I take notes, so that I won't forget.

6) *to take a picture*　　いっしょに写真をとりましょう。
Let's take a picture together.

Ⅲ. ⟨ffff⟩ 🐟 は: は used to develop a conversation

Look at the cartoons (A) and (B).

In discourse, a topic is often introduced as **[N] が**; once it is established, it is then talked about/referred as **[N] は**.

In cartoon (A), Suzuki-san starts the conversation with

あそこに女の人がいますね

女の人がいます establishes what he wants to talk about with his foreign friend. Once it has been established, **[N] が** becomes **[N] は** in the subsequent conversation, as in **あの人はだれですか** in the 3rd frame of (A).

This switch from **[N] が** to **[N] は** is also seen in cartoon (B). Suzuki-san has a stomach-ache, and starts the conversation with **おなかが……** (an elision of **おなかが痛い**).

Having been established as a topic, his stomach-ache is then referred to with **[N] は** (＝**おなかは**), as used by his girlfriend in the 4th frame.

まとめ

(A) (B)

B. Conversation

I．Summary of Conversational Strategies

1．Factual information

□ □ How to explain a procedure   ：まず、〜。次に、〜。それから、〜。
        ⇨L20 S-2   ：〜場合は、〜。〜する時は、〜。
                 ：〜て、〜て、〜とできあがり。

□ □ How to leave a message   ：じゃ、すみませんが、伝言おねがい
        ⇨L18 S-4   します。／できますか。

                        ＜message＞と │ 伝えてください。
                                      │ お伝えください。

2．Judgement

□ □ How to express an opinion   ：これ、〜 │ でしょうか。
        ⇨L20 S-4   │ かな／かしら。
                 −そうですね。〜んじゃないでしょうか。
                 −そうね。〜んじゃない。↗

3．Emotions

4．Actions

□ □ How to invite someone to go   ：今度の〈date〉、 │ おひまですか。
     somewhere   ⇨L17 S-1a   │ 予定ありませんか。
                                     │ 時間ありますか。

        ⇨L17 S-1b   〈place/activity〉に │ 行きませんか。
                                      │ 行かない。↗

                  あした映画に │ 行かない。↗
                                 │ 行きませんか。

□ □ How to accept an invitation   −ええ、ぜひ。／よろこんで。
        ⇨L17 S-2   ：今度の土曜、映画に行きませんか。
                 −土曜は、ちょっと。

□ □ How to decline an invitation   ：うん、ちょっと。〜し、〜し。
        ⇨L17 S-3a
        ⇨L17 S-3b

まとめ

119

☐ ☐ How to ring someone at home
⇨L18 S-1

　：もしもし、木村先生のお宅ですか。
　　　－はい、木村でございます。
　　　あ、あの、私、松見大学の山下と申し
　　　ますが。

☐ ☐ How to ask for the person you
want　　　　　⇨L18 S-2a

　：あの、Xさん、｜いらっしゃいますか。
　　　　　　　　　　｜お願いします。

☐ ☐ How to arrange to ring again
⇨L18 S-3a

　：何時ごろお帰り｜ですか。
　　　　　　　　　　｜になりますか。

　〈time〉ごろ、　　｜またお電話｜します。
　　そのころ　　　　｜　　　　　　｜いたします。

☐ ☐ How to pass on a message
⇨L18 S-6

　：〈time〉、〈person〉から
　　　　　｜電話があったよ。🄲
　　　　　｜お電話がありました。🄴

　〈message〉｜って。🄲
　　　　　　　｜と言ってました。🄴
　　　　　　　｜とおっしゃってました。🄴

☐ ☐ How to ask for something to
be done for you　⇨L20 S-3

　：〜んだけど｜〜てもらえる。↗
　　　　　　　　｜〜てくれない。↗

5. Social formulas

☐ ☐ How to express praise ⇨L19 S-2

　：わあ！おいしそうですね。
　　　あら、かわいいおじょうさんですね。
　　　おっ、すごい車だな。♂／(ね)♀　　🄲
　　　絵がおじょうずですね。

☐ ☐ Greetings　　　　　⇨まとめ5Ⅱ3

6. Communication strategies

How to start a conversation
⇨L19 S-1a

☐ ☐ （7）Visiting

　：ごめんください。
　　　（こんにちは／こんばんは。）
　　　－はい。どなたですか。
　　　山下です。

□ □　(8) Creating an opening　　　　：何(を)｜してんの。☺／して(い)るの。
　　　　　⇨L20 S-1a　　　　　　　　　　　♀
　　　　　　　　　　　　　　　　　　　　　｜して(い)るんですか。
　　　　　　　　　　　　　　：どう｜したの。☺
　　　　　　　　　　　　　　　　　　｜したんですか。🈂
　　　　　　　　　　　　　　　　　　｜なさったんですか。♀🈂

□ □　(9) Praising　　　　⇨L20 S-1b　：いいネクタイしているね。♂☺
　　　　　　　　　　　　　　　　　　　－そう。↗　どうも。
　　　　　　　　　　　　　　　　　　　どこで買ったの。↗

□ □　Talking about the weather　　　：また、雨ですね。今年はよく降りますね。
　　　　　　　　　⇨L20 S-1c

How to end a conversation

□ □　(4) On the phone　　⇨L18 S-5　：じゃ、失礼します。
　　　　　　　　　　　　　　　　　　ごめんください。
　　　　　　　　　　　　　　　　：もう、そろそろ（失礼します。）

□ □　(5) Visiting　　　　⇨L19 S-4　：きょうは、本当にありがとうござい
　　　　　　　　　　　　　　　　　　ました。
　　　　　　　　　　　　　　　　　　どうもごちそうさまでした。
　　　　　　　　　　　　　　　　　　－いいえ、何のおかまいもしません
　　　　　　　　　　　　　　　　　　で。

II. *Additional Information*

1. Functions of the negative form

In the model conversation of Lesson 17, Suzuki-san said 「**よかったら、リサさんと二人で来ない**↗」. The **来ない**↗ (negative question) does not have a negative meaning, but expresses an invitation. More politely, **来ませんか** can be used: ⇨L3GNⅤ

① A：**昼ご飯、いっしょに食べませんか。** 😊⬆➡

　　B：**ええ。食べようか。** 😊⬆➡

② A：**あした、映画見ない。** 😊➡

　　B：**うん。行こうか。** 😊➡

There are other expressions using negative forms that don't have negative meanings. Recall the words of a passer-by in Lesson 12, 「**歩いて行くより，バスで行った方がいいんじゃないかしら。**🚶」. **～んじゃない**↗ puts the speaker's opinion to the listener in question form. The polite form of **～じゃない**↗ is **～じゃありませんか**.

高いんじゃ | **ない。**↗
　　　　　　 | **ありませんか。**↗

Isn't it expensive?

～ない can occur twice in a sentence; 「**高くないんじゃない。**」 *It's not expensive, is it?*, **高くない** being the negative form of **高い**, and **～じゃない** indicating the speaker's opinion.

① A：**あした、漢字のテストがあるんじゃない。**↗
　　　Isn't there going to be Kanji test tomorrow?

　　B：**えっ。そうかしら。**🚶
　　　What?! Really?

② A：**ね。この部屋ちょっと暑いんじゃない。**↗
　　　Hey, don't you think this room is a bit hot?

　　B：**そうかな。**
　　　I guess so.

③ A：鈴木さん、きょうちょっと元気じゃないんじゃない。
《すずき》　　　　　　　　　《げんき》

Mr. Suzuki does not look so well today, does he.

B：そうね。どうしたのかしら。🧍

No, I wonder what's wrong.

2. Male and female speech

In plain style conversation, males and females characteristically use different endings; see the table below for a comparison.

《Rule 1》 Verbs and I-adjectives

Women tend to add わ after Verbs and i-Adjectives:

	Male	Female
見る《み》	見る	見るわ
見ない	見ない	見ないわ
見た	見た	見たわ
見なかった	見なかった	見なかったわ

まとめ

《Rule 2 》

The particles **ね** and **よ** are used by both men and women, but women tend to add **わ** before **ね** and **よ**.

〈Verbs〉

	Male	Female
見る	見るよ	見るわよ
見ない	見ないよ	見ないわよ
見た	見たよ	見たわよ
見なかった	見なかったよ	見なかったわよ

〈I-adjectives〉

	Male	Female
大きい	大きいよ	大きいわよ
大きくない	大きくないよ	大きくないわよ
大きかった	大きかったよ	大きかったわよ
大きくなかった	大きくなかったよ	大きくなかったわよ

《Rule 3》 Nouns and na adjectives

After nouns and **na** adjectives male casual speech uses **だ** instead of **です**, whereas women either omit **だ** or use **だわ**:

＜Verbs＞

	Male	Female
休みです	休みだ	休みだわ
休みではない	休みじゃない	休みじゃないわ
休みでした	休みだった	休みだったわ
休みではなかった	休みじゃなかった	休みじゃなかったわ

＜Na adjective＞

	Male	Female
有名です	有名だ	有名だわ
有名でした	有名だった	有名だったわ

《Rule 4》 んです

In mens' casual speech **なんだ** is used instead of **んです** whereas women use **なの**:

	Male	Female
有名なんです	有名なんだ	有名なの
休みなんです	休みなんだ	休みなの

まとめ

《Other expressions》

	Male	Female
〜でしょう	〜だろう	〜でしょう
〜かしら	〜かな	〜かしら

3. *Keego* expressions

敬語 can be used for a variety of purposes:

a. Asking a question（about the listener）

お元気ですか。	*How are you?*
お忙しいですか。	*Are you busy?*
ご存じですか。	*Do you know?*
お出かけですか。	*Are you going out?*
お読みになりましたか。	*Did you read it?*
ご注文なさいますか。	*Would you like to order?*
めしあがりませんか。	*How about (some food)?*

b. Making a request ⇨L14CN S-1/L23CN S-2

教えて｜くださいますか／ませんか。 *Would you please tell me?*
　　　｜いただけますか／ませんか。
　　　｜いただきたいんですが。

お伝え｜くださいますか／ませんか。 *Could you please tell him/her?*
　　　｜いただけますか／ませんか。
　　　｜いただきたいんですが。

c. Giving instructions ⇨L10GNⅦ

お待ち _ま	くださいい。	*Please wait.*
お入り _{はい}		*Please come in.*
おかけ		*Please take a seat.*

d. Offering to do something（for the listener）⇨L10GNⅧ/L16CN S-1

お手伝い _{て つだ}	します。	*I'll help you.*
	しましょう。	
	しましょうか。	*May I help you?*

e. Asking permission ⇨L10GNⅧ/L8CN S-3

うかがいたいんですが。	*May I ask you something?*
お借りできますか。	*May I borrow it?*
お電話してもよろしいですか。 _{でん わ}	*Would it be all right if I telephone you?*

---

4. Greetings

a. For going out

When a family member or acquaintance goes to school or work, he will say:

A	行ってきます。 _い	*I'm off.*
	行ってまいります。🈺	

(Lit., I'll go and come back).

B：行ってらっしゃい。	*Bye.*

（*Please go and come back.*）

気をつけて。 _き	*Take care!*

These expressions are used not only between family members but also between neighbours or people who work at the same company, or who have a sense of belonging to the 'same group'.

Note that さようなら， こんにちは or こんばんは are not used among family members.

b. When coming home, family members exchange the following:

  A：**ただいま。**   *I'm home (now).*

  B：**お帰りなさい。**   *Welcome home.*

c. Other greetings

 When starting a meal, the expressions are:

  A：**いただきます。**

  B：**どうぞ。**

When finishing the meal, **ごちそうさま（でした）** is used. The same expressions are also used by a guest to his host when treated to a meal.

---

5. Characteristics of casual-style expressions

 The characteristics of casual-style expressions can be divided into a number of groups, which are reviewed below:

a. Omission of particles

何してんの。 （＝**何をしているの。**）	*What are you doing?*	〈L20〉
どこ行くの。 （＝**どこへ行くの。**）	*Where are you going?*	〈L2〉
80円切手、1まい。 （＝**80円切手を1まい。**）	*(Give me) A 80 yen stamp.*	〈L2〉

b. Omission of predicate

80円切手、1まい。 （＝**80円切手、1まいください。**）	*(Give me) A 80 yen stamp.*	〈L2〉
私、ホット。 （＝**私、ホットにする。**）	*Hot (coffee) for me.*	〈L3〉
どこ行くの。 **ー東京。** （＝**東京へ行く。**）	*Where are you going?* *- Tokyo.*	

c. Insertion of ね, さ, etc.

縮小コピーする時はね、このボタンを押すんだ。　　　〈L20〉
しゅくしょう　　　　とき　　　　　　　　　　　　　お
When making a reduced copy, you push this button.

音楽会があるんだけどさ、来ない。↗　　　　　　　　〈L17〉
おんがくかい　　　　　　　　　　こ
We're giving a concert. Won't you come?

d. Shortening the last part

こすぎるかも。　　　　　*It might be too dark.*
　（＝こすぎるかもしれない。）

道があるでしょ。↗　　　*Surely there's a road?*　　　〈L12〉
みち
　（＝道があるでしょう。↗）

行きましょ。↗　　　　　*Let's go.*
い
　（＝行きましょう。↗）

e. Dropping the last part

もう一度やってみて。　　*Try again.*　　　　　　　　〈L20〉
いちど
　（＝もう一度やってみてください。）

薬を飲んだら。↗　　　　*How about taking some medicine?*
くすり　の
　（＝薬を飲んだらどうですか。↗）

f. Shortening the middle part

困ってたんですよ。　　　*I was in trouble.*　　　　　　〈L13〉
こま
　（＝困っていたんですよ。）

やってないの。↗　　　　*You aren't doing it?*　　　　　〈L8〉
　（＝やっていないの。↗）

もらってってください。　*Please take it.*　　　　　　　〈L9〉
　（＝もらっていってください。）

まとめ

g. Contractions

何_{なに}してんの。 （＝何してるの。）	*What are you doing?*	〈L20〉
わかんないな。 （＝わからないな。）	*I don't know.*	〈L5〉
すいません。 （＝すみません。）	*Sorry.*	〈L5〉
書_かいといて。 （＝書いておいて。）	*Write it.*	〈L15〉
酔_よっぱらっちゃった。 （＝酔っぱらってしまった。）	*(He's) drunk.*	〈L16〉
ＬＬっていうの。 （＝ＬＬというの。）	*so-called "LL".*	〈L10〉
上手_{じょうず}ってほどじゃない。 （＝上手というほどじゃない。）	*I'm not so good.*	〈L17〉

事務室_{じむしつ}へ取_とりに来_きてくださいって。　　　　　　　〈L5〉
It says "Please come and collect it."
（＝事務室へ取りに来てくださいということだ。）

第21課

苦情
くじょう
Complaining

OBJECTIVES:

Model Conversation

(1)

Characters : Yamashita(山下), a neighbour(隣の人 female)

Situation : Yamashita-san was writing a report until late at night. But there was a party next door. The noise was disturbing him, so he went to talk to the neighbour.

Flow-chart :

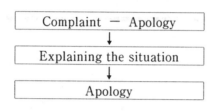

Complaint — Apology
↓
Explaining the situation
↓
Apology

―山下さんのアパートで―

山 下：(Knock-knock)

隣の人：はい。どなた。

山 下：すみません。隣の者ですけど。

隣の人：(The door opens) はい、何か。

山 下：あのう、すみませんが、もう少し静かにしてもらえませんか。

隣の人：あ、どうもすみません。

       *　　*　　*

隣の人：今、友達が集まって、ちょっとパーティーやってるもんですから。

山 下：あのう、もう11時をすぎてるんですけど。

隣の人：あ、そうか。気がつかなくて。

山 下：レポート書いているもんですから。
　　　　お願いします。

隣の人：はい。

       *　　*　　*

隣の人：どうもすみませんでした。これから気をつけます。

山 下：いいえ。どうも。

（2）

Characters ：Suzuki(鈴木), his landlady（大家）

Situation ：Suzuki-san meets his landlady in the street, and she cautions him about the refuse.

Flow-chart ：

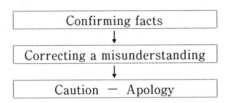

```
┌─────────────────────────────────┐
│       Confirming facts          │
└─────────────────────────────────┘
                ↓
┌─────────────────────────────────┐
│  Correcting a misunderstanding  │
└─────────────────────────────────┘
                ↓
┌─────────────────────────────────┐
│      Caution － Apology          │
└─────────────────────────────────┘
```

―鈴木さんのアパートで―

大　家：鈴木さん。

鈴　木：はい、何か。

大　家：あ、鈴木さん。けさ、ごみ出したでしょう。

鈴　木：ええ、8時前にちゃんといつものところに出しときましたけど。

大　家：それは、いいんだけど、あれ、もえないごみだったでしょう。

鈴　木：ええ。

$$* \qquad * \qquad *$$

鈴　木：水曜日はもえないごみの日じゃなかったんですか。

大　家：あら、ちがうのよ。
　　　　月、水、金はもえるごみ、もえないごみは、木曜でしょう。

鈴　木：え、そうだったんですか。

$$* \qquad * \qquad *$$

大　家：じゃ、今まで、ずっと間違えていたの。しょうがないわね。

鈴　木：はあ、どうもすみません。

大　家：きょうのは、私があずかっといたけど。
　　　　こういうことは、ちゃんとしてくれないと困るのよ。

鈴　木：はい。どうもご迷惑かけてすみませんでした。

大　家：じゃ、今度から木曜日に出すようにしてね。

鈴　木：はい。これから気をつけます。

MC

Report

　山下さんはきのうの晩レポートを書いていたが、隣の部屋のパーティがうるさくてなかなか書けなかった。それで、隣のドアをノックして、もう少し静かにするように頼んだ。隣の人は11時をすぎていることに気がついていなかった。夜遅くまで騒がれると迷惑だと思った。

　鈴木さんはもえるごみを出す日ともえないごみを出す日を間違えていた。鈴木さんは、水曜日はもえないごみの日だと思って、もえないごみを出してしまった。大家さんに月、水、金はもえるごみで、木曜日がもえないごみの日だと注意された。

New Words and Expressions

Words in the conversation

隣	となり	next door; neighbour
友だち	ともだち	friend
集まる	あつまる	to gather
すぎる		it's past (11 o'clock)
気がつく	き	to notice
これから		from now
気をつける		to pay attention
		to take care
大家	おおや	landlord; landlady
ごみ		trash
ちゃんと		properly; correctly; duly
いつものところ		usual place
もえるゴミ		combustible refuse
間違える	まちがえる	make a mistake
あずかる		to hold;
		look after something
迷惑	めいわく	a trouble; bother

<Expressions in the conversation>

どなた　　　　　　　　　　　*Who is it?*

どなたですか is a more polite expression. When someone knocks at the door, a person who is in the room or house replys どなたですか, In this case, one does not use だれですか.

何か。
なに

This is a way of asking what someone wants after having been addressed by あのう、すみません. 何ですか or 何でしょうか are more polite versions.

もう少し静かにしてもらえませんか。
　　　しず

This literally means *Please be a little more quiet.* ～してもらう is used to riquest an action.

パーティをやってるもんですから。

〜**もんだから** is a contracted form of 〜**もんですから**. It is used when making an excuse. ⇨CN

ちゃんといつものところに出しておきました

ちゃんと has various meanings. In this conversation **ちゃんと** has the nuance of doing something properly.

しょうがない

Similar **しかたがない**, this usually indicates that there is no choice, but in this conversation, **しょうがない** has the sense of "You are hopeless," blaming Yamashita-san for his error.

今日のは、私が預かっといた

〜**といた** is a contracted form of 〜**ておいた**.

Words in the report

なかなか		*not easily; not readily*
騒ぐ	さわぐ	*make a disturbance; be noisy*
注意する	ちゅういする	*warning; give advice*

Grammar Notes

I. 〜て〈3〉: *because* 〜

Examples

① 山田さんは病気で来られなかった。
やまだ　　　びょうき　こ
Yamada-san was unable to come because he was ill.

② この本は難しくてわからない。
　　ほん　むずか
This book is too difficult; I cannot understand it.

③ ここは静かでよく勉強できます。
　　　しず　　　　べんきょう
It's quiet here, so I can study well.

④ 遅くなってすみません。
　おそ
Sorry to be late. (lit. Sorry because I'm late.)

【*Explanation*】

1. General explanation of 〜て，〜

As we saw in Lesson 6, two or more sentences can be combined into one with the
-te form. ⇨ L6GNⅣ. Although the -te form itself does not have any meaning, and
merely serves to connect sentences. Therefore, a variety of meanings are implied
depending on the nature of the relation between the connected sentences:

(1) successive actions or events:

田中さんと食事しました。　　＋　　映画に行きました。
たなか　　しょくじ　　　　　　　えいが　い
I had a meal with Tanaka-san.　　　*I went to a movie.*

↓

田中さんと食事して、映画に行きました。
I had a meal with Tanaka-san and then went to a movie.

(2) simultaneous actions, the first being the means for accomplishing the second:

テープを聞きました。　　＋　　日本語を勉強しました。
I listened to the tape.　　　　　*I studied Japanese.*

↓

テープを聞いて、日本語を勉強しました。
I studied Japanese by listening to the tape.

(3) cause or reason

飲みすぎました。　　＋　　頭が痛いです。
I had too much to drink.　　　*I've got a headache.*

↓

飲みすぎて、頭が痛いです。
I had too much to drink, so I've got a headache.

2. -te form expressing cause or reason

1) Explanation

{S₁[-te]} ,　　　　{S₂}
cause/reason　　　response/result

ニュースを聞いて、びっくりしました。
Hearing the news, I got a shock.

When the action of {S₁} has already happened and {S₂} describes an emotional response to it, or a negative result/apology, the relation between the cause ({S₁}) and effect ({S₂}) is better expressed with 〜て (-te form) rather than 〜から or 〜ので. Note that the action or state of {S₂} is uncontrollable.

Following are some examples of appropriate expressions for {S₂}.

{S₁<cause/reason>}	{S₂<response/result>}	
安くて 会えて	〈adjectives of emotion〉 うれしい よかった	*I'm glad it's cheap.* *I'm glad to meet you.*

	〈verbs of emotion〉	
テレビを見_みて	おどろいた	*I was startled by what I saw on TV.*
むずかしくて	困_{こま}った	*It's so hard that I don't know what to do.*
	〈negative potential verbs〉	
病気_{びょうき}で	行けない	*I can't go because I'm sick.*
	〈apologies, thanks〉	
おそくなって	すみません	*I'm sorry to be late.*

2) Use in apologies and thanks

1. 遅_{おそ}くなって、すみません。　　*Sorry to be late.*

2. あした行_いけなくて、ごめんなさい。　*Sorry I can't make it tomorrow.*

3. 手伝_{てつだ}ってくれて、ありがとう。　*Thank you for your help.*

おそくなって
　　すみません。

II. The こ/そ/あ/ど system 〈3〉: the あ series for shared knowledge

---

Examples

① A：あれ、燃_もえないゴミだったでしょう。
   That was refuse which doesn't burn, wasn't it?

   B：ええ。
   That's right.

② A：あの問題は困りましたね。

That problem is troublesome, isn't it?

B：ほんとうに、困りましたね。

Yes, it really is a bother.

③ A：どこに食事に行きましょうか。

Where shall we go for a dinner?

B：このあいだ行ったところは。

How about the place we went last time?

A：ああ、あそこ、いいですね。

Oh, that place, fine.

【*Explanation*】

In Lesson 4, we saw that the あ column of the こ/そ/あ/ど series refers to items at a distance from speaker and listener. Here, we will look at the use of the あ column to refer to matters which are not in the field of vision of speaker/listener, but concern knowledge shared between them. You can see from the examples that both speaker and listener know what is being talked about and refer to it with あれ, あの, あそこ etc.

When either speaker or listener is unfamiliar with what is being talked about, it is referred to with the そ series instead; compare the pair of examples:

1.　A：木村先生の授業はどうですか。
きむらせんせい　じゅぎょう
What do you think about Kimura-sensee's class?

B：あれは大変ですよ。宿題がたくさんあるから。
たいへん　しゅくだい
It's a tough class, because we have so much homework.

2.　A：木村先生の授業はどうですか。
What do you think about Kimura-sensee's class?

B：それとってないんですけど。何の授業ですか。
なん
I am not attending it. Which class is it?

Ⅲ.　Use of ～ように: する verbs and なる verbs 〈5〉

GN

Examples

① A：英語で話さないようにしてください。
えいご　はな
Please make an effort not to speak in English.

B：はい、日本語で話すようにします。
に ほん ご
All right, I'll make an effort to speak in Japanese.

② 日本語の本が読めるようになりました。
ほん　よ
I can read Japanese books now.

③ リサさんが日本語の本が読めるように、漢字にひらがなをつけてあげました。
かん じ
I put Hiragana next to the Kanji so that Lisa-san can read the Japanese book.

【Explanation】

1.　～ようにする　vs　～ようになる

する *to do/make/change something* contrasts in meaning with なる *to become/be changed to.*

する and the so-called する verbs describe actions that can be carried out of one's own will, so even if no actor is mentioned, the implication is that someone is responsible for the action. On the other hand, なる and なる verbs imply that any actor is being ignored/doesn't exist (i.e. things happen naturally); they focus on (a change of) state. ⇨L9GNⅤ，L11GNⅢ

When someone is responsible for a change, する is used:

1. **ワインにする。**

   (Someone) makes (grapes) into wine.

2. **赤くする。**

   (Someone) makes (something) red.

3. **先生は学生が上手に話せるようにした。**

   The teacher got the students to speak fluently.

4. **たばこをすわないようにする。**

   I'll make an effort not to smoke.

Thus, [V-(r)u] **ようにする** means *to make an effort to* ～, and [V-nai] **ようにする**, *to make an effort not to* ～.

When the focus is on a state resulting from a change (or when it doesn't matter who made the change), **なる** is used:

1. **ワインになる。**

   (Grapes) change to wine.

2. **赤くなる。**

   (Something) becomes red.

3. **学生が上手に話せるようになった。**

   The students have become able to speak well.

4. **たばこをすわないようになった。**

   (Someone) is not smoking any more.

5. **歩けるようになった。**

   (The baby) has become able to walk.

～ようになる, therefore, means *to get to the stage where* ～ as a result of a natural development.

赤くする

赤くなる

ワインにする

ワインになる

話せるようにする

話せるようになる

たばこをすう

すわないようにする

すわないようになる

歩けない

歩けるようになる

When you describe any changes using **する** or **なる**, choose an appropriate one from the structures shown in the table below.

[V-(r)u] ように [V-nai] ように [A-ku] [NA] に [N] に	する なる

2. ～ようにしてください

～ようにしてください *please make an effort to* ... is used to express a request which requires the listener to make an effort.

1. **忘れないようにしてください。**
   _{わす}
   Please make an effort/make sure not to forget it.

2. **お金を使いすぎないようにしてください。**
   _{かね} _{つか}
   Please make an effort not to spend too much money.

3. **あしたは早く起きるようにして。**
   _{はや} _お
   Please get up early tomorrow.

For requests, **忘れないでください，使いすぎないでください** and **起きてください** can also be used, but these requests are more direct than those using **～ようにしてください**.

～ようにしてください can be attached to the forms shown below.

[V-(r)u] [V-nai]	ように してください

3. ～ように、～

Look at the following examples below using, {S₁} **ように**, {S₂}. We saw that **～ようにする** implies making an effort; in {S₁} you describe the effort to make and in {S₂} you explain what arrangements you made to make that effort successful:

1. **忘れないようにノートに書いた。**
   I wrote it in my notebook so that I won't forget.

2. **お金を使いすぎないように2000円だけさいふに入れた。**
   I put only 2000 yen in my wallet so that I won't spend too much money.

3. **あしたは早く起きられるようにきょうは早く寝よう。**
   I'll go to bed early so that I can get up early tomorrow.

GN

This structure is used as shown below.

$$\left\{ S_1 \begin{array}{c} [V-(r)u] \\ [V-nai] \end{array} \right\} ように、\{S_2\}$$

Conversation Notes

\<General Information\>

1. Refuse collection

Collecting refuse is a complicated business in Japan. When you put out refuse, you usually have to separate it into combustible (**燃えるごみ**) and non-combustible (**燃えないごみ**) items, and take it to the nearest collection area on the fixed day or date. Some areas also have separate collections for bottles and for bulk garbage two or three times a month. Check with your landlord/landlady (**大家さん**), a neighbour, or the local townhall about how refuse collection is handled in your area.

燃えるごみ
(combustible)

燃えないごみ
(non-combustible)

粗大ごみ
(bulk garbage)

資源ごみ
(recyclable refuse)

水銀電池
(mercury battery)

146

2. Refering to people

When introducing yourself, you usually give your name. In some situations, however, it may be more appropriate to identify yourself in a different way:

① 隣の者ですが、もう少し静かにしてください。
I am the person next door. Can you be a little quieter?

② 筑波大の学生ですが、アンケートをお願いします。
I am a student of the University of Tsukuba.
Please answer the questionnaire.

If you know someone's name you can call him/her by the surname plus title: ～先生 *teacher, professor* ～部長 *department head* (in a company), etc., or surname plus ～さん:

① 木村先生に相談して決めます。
I'll decide after consulting with Prof. Kimura.

② 山田部長といっしょに行ってください。
Please go with the Head of the Department, Mr/Ms Yamada.

How do you refer to someone whose name you don't know? You can use ～人, ～方 as follows. ～方 is a polite equivalent of ～人.

① あそこにいる人に聞きます。
I'll ask the person over there.

② この方が助けてくださいました。
This gentleman/lady helped me.

You may have experience being called お客さん, in a store or on a bus. The word お客さん *(visitor)* can be used to refer to a customer or a passenger.

① お客さん、忘れ物ですよ。
You've left something, sir.

② お客さん、あぶないですよ。電車がきますから。
Here comes a train, sir. Be careful!

CN

＜*Strategies*＞

S-1. How to complain

a. Implicit complaints

When something annoys you, you might want to complain about it – but how? You can indicate your complaint in a variety of polite (indirect) ways:

| あのう | 申しわけありませんが、
すみませんが | テレビの音が （……）。 |

lit. Excuse me, but the sound of the TV is...

An unfinished sentence like the above is often used in Japan, but to the higher you can also complain by first indicating your situation, and gradually bringing up your complaint:

🔊 A：あのう、今、論文を書いているんですけど……。
I'm writing my thesis, but ...

B：はい。　　　　　　　　　*Yes?*

A：ちょっとテレビの音が……。
The sound of the TV is a bit ...

B：ああ、すみません。大きかったですか。
Oh, I'm sorry. Was it too loud?

A：ええ。お願いします。　　*Yes, please.*

When the other party doesn't realize what you are complaining about, you can complain more directly:

A：あのう、ちょっとテレビの音が。

B：え、テレビの音が何か。↗

A：もう少し、小さくしていただけないでしょうか。
今、論文書いているもんですから。

B：ああ、すみません。気がつかなくて。

A：お願いします。

b. Explicit complaints

To a close friend, you can complain more directly:

A：あのう、悪いんだけど。

B：何か。↗

A：テレビの音、もう少し、小さくして ｜ くれないかな。
　　　　　　　　　　　　　　　　　　　　｜ もらえないかな。

Would you mind turning it down a little?

B：あ、ごめん。気がつかなくて。　　*Sorry. I hadn't realized.*

S-2. How to express anger

When someone wants to show his/her anger, s/he may use the following terms:

CN

a.

頭に来るわ。　　
頭に来るよ。

They really make me mad!

b.

冗談いわないでよ。
冗談いうなよ。

You've got to be kidding.

c.

いいかげんにしてよ。
いいかげんにしろよ。

Give me a break!

d.

ほっといてよ。
ほっといてくれよ。

Leave me alone.

149

e.

やめてよ。 ♀
やめろよ。 ♂
Cut it out.

何するのよ。 ♀
何するんだよ。 ♂
What are you doing.

There are different levels of formality for the word *you* in Japanese. At the formal end of the scale is **あなた** and **おまえ／おめえ，てめえ**（♂）will be use in cases of extreme anger.

S-3. How to admit a mistake

Mistakes often happen through lack of understanding Japanese. For example, in the model conversation Suzuki-san made a mistake about the day of collection so he was cautioned about it by **大家さん**（landlady）.

鈴木：水曜日は、もえないごみの日じゃなかったんですか。

大家：あら、ちがうのよ。
　　　月、水、金はもえるごみ、もえないごみは、木曜でしょう。↗

鈴木：え、そうだったんですか。↗

You can use **そうだったんですか**（*Is that right?*）when your Japanese is corrected or when you made a mistake in everyday life. You can add **すみません。これから気をつけます。**

A：ミーティングは、10時からじゃなくて、9時からだったんですよ。

B：えっ。そうだったんですか。
　　すみません。これから気をつけます。

S-4. How to apologize —2.

We have seen some expressions conveying apology:

申し訳ありません。🔲
申し訳ない。ⓒ♠
すみません。
すまん。ⓒ♠
ごめんなさい。ⓒ
ごめん。ⓒ➡⬇

もうしわけありません（*lit. I have no excuse.*）is more formal than **すみません**, but both expressions are often repeated several times with much bowing, 'hissing' and facial expressions of regret.

Other common expressions are:

悪いですね。🔲
悪いわね。♠　／悪いな。♠ⓒ
悪い！ⓒ

悪いですね and **ごめんなさい** are used for apologizing like **すいません**, but have a more familiar ring than **もうしわけありません** or **すいません**.

① A : 悪い！｜また、約束の時間におくれちゃって。
　　　ごめん！｜
　　Sorry to be late again!

　 B : ほんとうに。しょうがないわね。
　　Really! You're hopeless, aren't you.

You can also explain the reason why you are doing something that is causing a complaint, using **〜もんですから**: ⇨L13 S-1b

② A : あのう、すいません。

　 B : はい。何でしょう。↗

　 A : せんたく機の音が……
　　The sound of the washing machine ...

B：あ、すみません。
じつは、ひるまずっと働いている │ もんですから。
│ ので……。
│ んです。

I am working all day, so ...

A：そうですか。でも、もう1時すぎですよ。

B：あと30分で終わりますから。すみません。
I'll be ready in 30 minutes.

A：30分ですね。お願いしますよ。

When you hadn't realized that you annoyed someone, apologize with 気がつかなくて、すみません or これから気をつけます.

A：あのう。もう少し、静かに歩いていただけませんか。
Will you please walk more quietly?

B：えっ？ ↗

A：下はうるさいんですよ。
There is a lot of noise from upstairs.

B：すみません。気がつかなくて。
これから、気をつけます。

The above situation is not unusual, because ordinary Japanese apartment houses are not sound-proofed.

お見舞い
みま
Visiting a sick person

OBJECTIVES:

GRAMMAR

I. Causative sentences
II. 〜てしまう: completion of action
III. 〜らしい: *looks like 〜 / seems 〜*
IV. 〜んじゃないかと思う: *might 〜*
V. あと＋〈length of time/quantity〉: *another 〜*

CONVERSATION

＜General Information＞
1. Etiquette for visiting a sick person
2. Condolences and celebration

＜Strategies＞
S-1. How to start a conversation —9. Visiting a sick person
S-2. How to give a present
S-3. How to ask about the patient's condition: symptoms, progress, how long it will take, etc.
S-4. How to cheer up the patient
S-5. Asking someone to be more careful

Model Conversation

Characters ：Suzuki(鈴木)， Tanaka(田中)， Lisa Brown(リサ・ブラウン)

Situation ：Suzuki-san is in hospital after a traffic accident. Tanaka-san and Lisa-san visit him with flowers and a music tape.

Flow-chart ：

```
┌─────────────────────────────────────┐
│             Greetings                │        In the sickroom
└─────────────────────────────────────┘
                  ↓
┌─────────────────────────────────────┐
│           Giving a present           │
└─────────────────────────────────────┘
                  ↓
┌─────────────────────────────────────┐
│  Asking about the patient's condition│
└─────────────────────────────────────┘
                  ↓
┌─────────────────────────────────────┐
│            Saying good bye           │
└─────────────────────────────────────┘
```

―病室で―

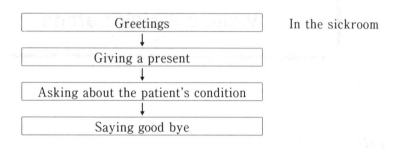

二　人：(Knock-knock) 失礼します。

鈴　木：やあ、これはどうも。

リ　サ：どうですか、具合いは。

鈴　木：いやあ、足の骨、折っちゃってね。

リ　サ：大変でしたね。

田　中：でも、お元気そうですね。

　　　　　＊　　　　＊　　　　＊

リ　サ：あの、これ、お見舞いなんですけど。

鈴　木：いや、これはどうも。

田　中：あ、じゃ、ちょっとこれ、花びんに入れてくるわね。

リ　サ：ええ。(Tanaka leaves the room)

　　　　　＊　　　　＊　　　　＊

鈴　木：これ、音楽のテープ。

リ　サ：ええ。たいくつしてるんじゃないかと思って。

鈴　木：いやあ、どうもすみません。

リ　サ：スティービー・ワンダーなんです。
　　　　　たまには、ポップスもいいんじゃないかと思って。

鈴　木：うれしいなあ。どうもありがとう。

154

リ　サ：鈴木さん、自転車に乗ってたんですって。
鈴　木：うん。
リ　サ：気をつけてくださいね。自転車もあぶないから。
鈴　木：いや、向こうが悪いんだよ。信号無視なんだから。
リ　サ：そうですか。びっくりしたでしょう。
鈴　木：うん。もうだめかと思ったよ。
リ　サ：まだ痛むんですか。
鈴　木：うん、少しね。
　　　　でも、単純骨折だからすぐなおるって、医者が言ってた。
リ　サ：で、いつごろ退院できるんですか。
鈴　木：あと一週間ぐらいかな。
リ　サ：そうですか。

　　　　　　＊　　　　＊　　　　＊

田　中：じゃ、そろそろ失礼しましょうか。
リ　サ：そうね。
鈴　木：あれ、もう帰っちゃうの。残念だなあ。
リ　サ：ごめんなさい。これからゼミがあるんです。
田　中：それに、あまり疲れさせても悪いし。
鈴　木：そうか。じゃ、きょうは本当にありがとう。
田　中：じゃ、どうぞお大事に。
リ　サ：お大事に。
鈴　木：どうも。

MC

Report

＜田中さんの日記＞

　鈴木さんが交通事故にあって入院していると聞いて、病院へお見舞いに行った。リサさんがいっしょだったので、すごくうれしそうだった。鈴木さんには何よりの薬だろう。足のほねが折れてしまったと言っていたが、わりに元気そうで安心した。自転車に乗っていて車にぶつけられた時は、もうだめなんじゃないかと思ったという話だったが、一週間ぐらいで退院できるそうだ。たくさん話したので、疲れさせたかもしれない。

New Words and Expressions

Words in the conversation

病室	びょうしつ	*hospital room*
具合い	ぐあい	*condition* ＝調子（ちょうし）
足	あし	*leg, foot*
骨	ほね	*bone*
折る	おる	*to break*
お見舞い	おみまい	*visit and/or gift*
	cf. お見舞いに行く	*to visit a sick person*
	お見舞いの手紙を書く	*to write a get-well letter*
花びん	かびん	*vase*
入れる	いれる	*to put into*
たいくつする		*to get bored*
スティービー・ワンダー		name of a pop singer
たまには		*occasionally*
ポップス		*pop music*
うれしい		*glad, happy*
自転車	じてんしゃ	*bicycle*
あぶない		*dangerous*
向こう	むこう	*the other party*
信号無視	しんごうむし	*ignoring a red light*
びっくりする		*to be surprised* ＝おどろく
痛む	いたむ	*to have a pain, to ache*
単純骨折	たんじゅんこっせつ	*simple fracture*
なおる		*to be cured*
退院する	たいいんする	*to be discharged*
あと一週間	あといっしゅうかん	*one more week*
それに		*besides, moreover*
疲れさせる	つかれさせる	*to make someone tired*

156

<Expressions in the conversation>

これはどうも　　　　　　　　　　　　　　*Thank you for coming.*
　　When receiving an unexpected visit, **これはどうも** is used instead of **いらっ
　　しゃい**. **これはどうも** can also be used when receiving an unexpected gift.

どうですか、具合いは。　　　　　　　　　*Your condition — how is it?*
　　This is an inverted sentence for **具合いは、どうですか**.

足の骨、折っちゃってね。　　　　　　　　*I broke my leg.*
　　＝足の骨（を）折ってしまいましてね。 🈁 ～してしまう ⇨L22GNⅡ
　　cf. 骨を折る＝骨折する *to break a bone*

大変でしたね。　　　　　　　　　　　　　*You've had a hard time.*

気をつけてくださいね。　　　　　　　　　*Take care.*

びっくりしたでしょう。 ↗　　　　　　　　*You must have been surprised.*
　　　　～でしょう ⇨L19GNⅠ

もうだめかと思ったよ。　　　　　　　　　*I thought it was all over.*

もう帰っちゃうの。　　　　　　　　　　　*Are you leaving already?*
　　＝もう帰ってしまうんですか。 🈁 ～してしまう ⇨L22GNⅡ

ごめんなさい。　　　　　　　　　　　　　*Sorry.*

どうぞお大事に。　　　　　　　　　　　　*Get well soon.*

Words in the report

交通事故	こうつうじこ	*a traffic accident*
入院する	にゅういんする	*to be in a hospital*
すごく		*very*
ぶつける		*to hit (a car, etc.)*

<Expressions in the report>

何より　　　　　　　　　　　　　　　　*above all*
　① 何よりのものをありがとうございます。
　　　Thank you very much for such a wonderful gift.
　② 何より困ったのは、住むところでした。
　　　The biggest problem was where to live.

MC

③ お元気で何よりです。
I'm so glad you are well.

わりに　　　　　　　　　　　　　　　　　　*considering*

① むすこは３年生ですが、わりに大きいんです。
My son is in the 3rd grade, but he is big (for his age).

② Ａ：私はそうじがきらいなんです。
I hate cleaning.

Ｂ：そうですか。そのわりには、きれいな部屋ですね。
Really? Considering that, your room is tidy.

〜という話だ　　　　　　　　　*I heard the story that 〜*
　　〜という ⇨L11GNⅣ　　　**＝〜そうだ** ⇨L19GNⅢ

① 田中さんは結婚したという話だ。
I heard (the story) that Tanaka got married.

② もうだめなんじゃないかと思ったという話だった。
I heard that he thought it was all over.

Grammar Notes

Ⅰ. Causative sentences

Examples

① **先生が学生を立たせます。**
せんせい がくせい た
The teacher makes the students stand up.

② **先生が学生に本を読ませます。**
ほん よ
The teacher makes the students read a book.

③ **お手伝いさせてください。**
てつだ
Let me help you.

④ **あした休ませていただきたいんですが。**
やす
I'd like your permission to be absent tomorrow.

【*Explanation*】

Sentences like ① and ② are called causative sentences, because they indicate that someone (the causer) makes someone else (the causee) do something. Causatives can, however, also indicate that someone permits someone else to do something - this use of causative verbs is called 'permissive'.

The structure of causative sentences is as follows.

1. を causative for 《－を verb》（①）

Where a 《－を verb》 takes the particle が, the corresponding causative verb takes を:

先生 *The teacher*
せんせい
↘

（<u>学生が立つ</u>）
　がくせい　た
A student stands up.

↓

（Causative）　**先生が　学生を　立たせる。**
The teacher makes a student stand up.

↓

（Result）　**学生が立つ。** *A student stands up.*

1. **私が子どもを銀行へ行かせる。**
   わたし　こ　　　ぎんこう　い
   I make my child go to the bank.

→ **子どもが銀行へ行く。**
My child goes to the bank.

2. **アニルさんが友だちを笑わせる。**
   　　　　　とも　　わら
   Anil-san makes his friends laugh.

→ **友だちが笑う。**
Anil-san's friends laugh.

3. **子どもがリサさんをびっくりさせた。**
   A child gave Lisa-san a fright.

→ **リサさんがびっくりした。**
Lisa-san got a fright.

2. に causative 《＋を verb》（②）

Where a 《＋を verb》 takes the particle が, the corresponding causative verb takes に:

先生 *The teacher*
せんせい

（学生が本を読む）
　がくせい　ほん　よ
A student reads a book.

（Causative）　先生が　　学生を　本を　読ませる。
　　　　　　　せんせい　　　　　　　　　　に

The teacher makes a student read a book.

（Result）　学生が本を読む。　*A student reads a book.*

1. 先生が学生に仕事を手伝わせる。　→　学生が仕事を手伝う。
　　　　　　　しごと　てつだ　　　　　　　　　　　　しごと　てつだ
The teacher makes a student help him with his work.　*The student helps with his teacher's work.*

2. （私が）弟にまどを開けさせた。　→　弟がまどを開けた。
　　わたし　おとうと　　あ　　　　　　　　　　　　　　あ
I made my younger brother open the window.　*My younger brother opened the window.*

3. （私が）妹に車を洗わせた。　→　妹が車を洗った。
　　　　いもうと　くるま　あら　　　　　　　　　　あら
I made my younger sister wash the car.　*My younger sister washed the car.*

In a causative sentence, the causer（＝ the subject）takes が（は when topicalized）, whereas the causee takes に with 《＋を verb》, and を with 《一を verb》.

Now, who do you think made whom wash the car in the following?

（1）アニルさんに車を洗わせました。

（2）アニルさんが車を洗わせました。

Ans. (2) Anil-san made me/someone wash the car.

Ans. (1) I/Someone made Anil-san wash the car.

	Causative verbs			
Ordinary verbs	Non-past pos.	Non-past neg.	Past pos.	Past neg.
Group Ⅰ	**-u → -aseru**			
iku　*to go* 行く	ikaseru 行かせる	ikasenai 行かせない	ikaseta 行かせた	ikasenakatta 行かせなかった
nomu　*to drink* 飲む	nomaseru 飲ませる	nomasenai 飲ませない	nomaseta 飲ませた	nomasenakatta 飲ませなかった
toru　*to take* とる	toraseru とらせる	torasenai とらせない	toraseta とらせた	torasenakatta とらせなかった
matsu　*to wait* 待つ	mataseru 待たせる	matasenai 待たせない	mataseta 待たせた	matasenakatta 待たせなかった
kau　*to buy* 買う	kawaseru 買わせる	kawasenai 買わせない	kawaseta 買わせた	kawasenakatta 買わせなかった
Group Ⅱ	**-ru → -saseru**			
taberu　*to eat* 食べる	tabesaseru 食べさせる	tabesasenai 食べさせない	tabesaseta 食べさせた	tabesasenakatta 食べさせなかった
miru　*to see* 見る	misaseru 見させる	misasenai 見させない	misaseta 見させた	misasenakatta 見させなかった
akeru　*to open* 開ける	akesaseru 開けさせる	akesasenai 開けさせない	akesaseta 開けさせた	akesasenakatta 開けさせなかった
Group Ⅲ				
kuru　*to come* 来る	kosaseru 来させる	kosasenai 来させない	kosaseta 来させた	kosasenakatta 来させなかった
suru　*to do* する	saseru させる	sasenai させない	saseta させた	sasenakatta させなかった
shinpai suru 心配する　*to worry*	shinpai saseru 心配させる	shinpai sasenai 心配させない	shinpai saseta 心配させた	shinpai sasenakatta 心配させなかった

Causative verbs conjugate like Group Ⅱ verbs:

行かせる　　　　　　行かせて
行かせない　　　　　　行かせます
行かせた
行かせなかった

2. Causative verbs vs ～てもらう／～ていただく

Note that the causer is usually superior in status to the causee, because making someone else do something implies authority. Therefore, causative verbs are not normally used when a person of inferior status gets an equal or a superior to do something; instead, ～てもらう／～ていただく are used.（Pay attention to the particles used in ～てもらう／～ていただく sentence）:

（inappropriate）　　　**友だちを銀行へ行かせた。**
（appropriate）　　　　**友だちに銀行へ行ってもらった。**
I had my friend go to the bank.

（inappropriate）　　　**私たちは先生に本を読ませました。**
（appropriate）　　　　**私たちは先生に本を読んでいただきました。**
We had the teacher read a book.

You can however make very polite permissive sentences by combining causative verbs with verbs of giving and receiving:

1. **友だちのワープロを使わせてもらいました。**
   I was allowed to use my friend's word processor.

2. **事務室でコピー機を使わせてくれた。**
   They allowed us to use the photocopier in the office.

3. **先生の論文を読ませていただきました。**
   I was allowed to read my teacher's article.

4. **授業を休んだ友だちにコピーをとらせてあげた。**
   I let my friend, who missed the class, make a copy (of my notebook).

The following 1) and 2) are very similar in meaning; you can use either to get permission from a superior.

1) -te form of causative verb ＋ **くださいませんか**

    5. 写真をとらせてください。
        Allow me to take a photo, please.

    6. その仕事をぼくにやらせてくださいませんか。
        Would you let me do that job?

2) -te form of causative verb ＋ **ほしい、もらえる／いただける、もらいたい／いただきたい**

    7. コピーをとらせてほしいんですが。
        May I take a copy?

    8. 写真をとらせてもらえませんか。
        Would you let me take a photo?

    9. その仕事をぼくにやらせていただけませんか。
        Won't you let me do that job?

    10. あした休ませてもらいたいんですが。
         May I be absent tomorrow.

    11. 午前中で帰らせていただきたいんですが。
         May I be allowed to go home by noon.

Can you guess who will wash the car in the following sentences?

    （1）　アニルさん、車を洗ってくださいませんか。

    （2）　アニルさん、車を洗わせてくださいませんか。

Ans. (2) I/We will wash the car.

Ans. (1) Anil-san will wash the car.

3) If you want to ask permission to be absent tomorrow, you can use any of the expressions below. (Those on the left do not use causative forms, the ones on the right do. Politeness increases the further down you go.) ⇨L8GNⅧ

	Causative ＋ ～
あした休ませて…	あした休ませてください。 あした休ませて ｜ もらえ / いただけ ｜ ませんか。*
あした休んでもいいですか。	あした休ませて ｜ もらっ / いただい ｜ てもいいですか。
あした休みたいんですが。	あした休ませて ｜ もらい / いただき ｜ たいんですが。

　　* You can also use positive forms like くださいますか／もらえますか／いただけますか, but they are less polite than negative forms.

Ⅱ．～てしまう: completion of action

Examples

① ケーキを全部食べてしまいました。　　*I ate the whole cake.*
　　ぜんぶ　た

② 鈴木さんはよっぱらってしまいました。　　*Suzuki-san got drunk.*
　　すずき

③ 田中さんもよっぱらっちゃった。　　*Tanaka-san got drunk, too.*
　　たなか

【Explanation】

[V-te] しまう

食べてしまう 〕
　　　　　　　　 → 食べてしまいます
行ってしまう 〕　　　～てしまってください
　い　　　　　　　　 ～てしまったほうがいい
　　　　　　　　　　 ～てしまおう
　　　　　　　　　　 ～てしまえ

1. Use of ～てしまう

1) ～てしまう can express completion of an action *to... (do) completely.*

ケーキを全部食べてしまいました。　*I ate the whole cake.*

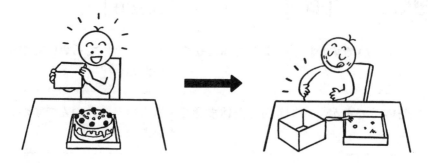

食べた can also indicate completion of an action, but 食べてしまった emphasizes completion.

1. **この本はもう読んでしまいました。**
   I've already finished (reading) this book.

2. **あしたまでにレポートを書いてしまいます。**
   I'll finish (writing) my report by tomorrow.

3. **早く宿題をやってしまおうと思います。**
   I intend to finish my homework quickly.

2) ～てしまう can also imply that the action has a result that is unfortunate for the speaker:

バスが行ってしまいました。　　　*The bus has gone.*

1. **パスポートをなくしてしまいました。**　*I lost my passport.*

2. **テープレコーダがこわれてしまった。**　*The tape recorder broke.*

2. Shortened forms of ～てしまう

These are commonly used conversationally:

		Shortened form of ～てしまう	
		Plain form	Polite form
Non-past	行ってしまう	行っちゃう	行っちゃいます
Past	行ってしまった	行っちゃった	行っちゃいました
Non-past	飲んでしまう	飲んじゃう	飲んじゃいます
Past	飲んでしまった	飲んじゃった	飲んじゃいました

1. A：バス、もう行ってしまいましたか。　　*Has the bus gone already?*

　　B：ええ、いま行っちゃいましたよ。　　*Yes, it just left.*

2. A：どうしたの。　　*What's the matter?*

　　B：パスポートなくしちゃったんだ。　　*I've lost my passport.*

3. A：本、持ってきた。　　*Did you bring the book?*

　　B：ごめん。忘れちゃった。　　*Sorry, I forgot.*

Ⅲ. ～らしい: *looks like/seems*

Examples

① こんばん台風が来るらしいです。
It seems that a typhoon will come tonight.

② その映画はおもしろいらしいです。
That movie sounds interesting.

③ こんどの試験は簡単らしいですよ。
It seems the next examination will be easy.

【*Explanation*】

らしい *apparently, it seems,* indicates that what you're saying is based on what you've heard or read, or on observation. Unlike そうだ（⇨L17GNⅢ）, which relies on observation only, and そうだ（⇨L19GNⅢ）, which expresses hearsay, らしい relies on information the speaker has heard, read or seen, and on judgements s/he has formed based on such information.

らしい inflects like [A]; it is attached to plain forms except in sentences ending in [N]＋だ and [NA]＋だ.（See * in the table below.）

[V]	書く、書いた、書かない 書かなかった、書いている 書いていない、……	
[A]	おもしろい おもしろくない おもしろかった おもしろくなかった	らしい
[NA]	元気* 元気じゃない 元気だった 元気じゃなかった	
[N]	休み* 休みじゃない 休みだった 休みじゃなかった	

Compare the following sentences.

1. a. このケーキはおいし<u>そう</u>です。 　　*This cake looks tasty.*

　 b. このケーキはおいしい<u>そう</u>です。 　　*I heard that this cake is tasty.*

　 c. このケーキはおいしい<u>らしい</u>です。 　　*It seems that this cake is tasty.*

2. a. 雪が降りそうです。　　　*It looks like it will snow.*
   ゆき ふ

 b. 雪が降るそうです。　　　*I heard that it will snow.*
    ふ

 c. 雪が降るらしいです。　　*It seems that it will snow.*
    ふ

> ### Ⅳ. ～んじゃないかと思う: *might* ～
>   おも

Examples

① 田中さんは行くんじゃないかと思う。
   た なか   い
   I think Tanaka-san might go.

② A：セーターを持ってきたんですか。
           も
   Did you bring a sweater?

   B：ええ、山の上は寒いんじゃないかと思って。
         やま うえ さむ
   Yes, I did. I thought it might be cold at the top of the mountain.

③ 大学に来ないから、病気なんじゃないかと思って心配していました。
   だいがく こ   びょうき   しんぱい
   Because you didn't come to university, I was worried that you might be ill.

GN

【*Explanation*】

　～んじゃないかと思う is similar to ～だろうと思う in meaning, but indicates less certainty. Compare the sentences:

（1）田中さんは<u>行く</u>と思う。　　　*I think Tanaka-san will go.*

（2）田中さんは<u>行くだろう</u>と思う。　*I think Tanaka-san may/will go.*

（3）田中さんは<u>行くんじゃないか</u>と思う。*I think Tanaka-san might go.*

　～んじゃないか uses a negative form, but does not give the sentence a negative meaning; it indicates uncertainty about the likelihood of something happening.

　Note how （4）differs in meaning from （3）above:

（4）田中さんは<u>行かないんじゃないか</u>と思う。*I think Tanaka-san might not go.*
　　　　（＝行かないだろう）

Let's look once more at ①～③, and the examples below:

1. <u>たいくつしているんじゃないかと思って</u>、（音楽テープを持ってきた。）
   I thought you might be bored, (so I brought a music tape.)

2. たまにはポップスも<u>いいんじゃないかと思って</u>、（スティービー・ワン
   ダーのテープを持ってきた。）
   *I thought it might be nice for you to listen to some pop music occasionally, (so
   I brought a Stevie Wonder tape).*

With the exception of ［N］＋だ and ［NA］＋だ，～んじゃないかと思う is
attached to plain forms. With ［N］ and ［NA］，な rather than だ is attached（see ＊ in
the table below）. ⇨L7GNⅡ

［V］	来る、来た、来ない 来なかった、来ている 来ていない、……	
［A］	遠い 遠くない 遠かった 遠くなかった	んじゃないかと思う
［NA］	不便な＊ 不便じゃない 不便だった 不便じゃなかった	
［N］	病気な＊ 病気じゃない 病気だった 病気じゃなかった	

3. このアパートは駅から遠いから、<u>不便なんじゃないかと思います</u>が。
   *Because this apartment is far from the station, I think it might be
   inconvenient.*

Ⅴ．あと＋＜length of time/quantity＞: *another ~*

あと＋＜length of time/quantity＞ is used to express the idea of *another ⟨length of time/quantity⟩*.

1. あと一週間で退院できる。
   Another week, and I'll be discharged/can go home from the hospital.

2. あと10日で私の誕生日だ。
   Another 10 days and it's my birthday.

3. A：木村先生は。
   Where is Kimura-sensee?

   B：いま授業です。あと10分したら授業は終わりますが。
   He's teaching now. The class will be over in another 10 minutes.

4. A：みんないますか。
   Is everyone here?

   B：あとアニルさんとリサさんがいません。
   Anil-san and Lisa-san are the only ones missing.
   (when they come, the group will be complete.)

5. A：もっと、ビール、くれよ。
   Give me some more beer.

   B：もうだめよ。
   No, you mustn't drink any more.

   A：じゃ、あと1本だけ。
   All right then, just one more bottle.

   B：ううん、じゃ、あと1本だけよ。
   Hmm... OK then - one only!

171

Conversation Notes

<General Information>

1. Etiquette for visiting a sick person

a. Visiting

Before visiting someone who is in hospital, you need to check the hospital's visiting hours (**面会時間**). At the hospital you normally fill in a form at the reception, writing the patient's name and room number, your name and address, your relation with the patient, the time of your visit, etc. When the sign on the door of the room says **面会謝絶** (*No visitors allowed*), you cannot see the patient.

面会者名簿				
月日	患者名	面会者名	続柄	面会時間
2月10日	鈴木　正	田中みどり	友人	2:00~2:40
〃	〃	リサ・ブラウン	〃	〃

b. Presents for sick persons

In Japan, a present for a sick person (**お見舞い**) is a must; flowers and assortments of fruit are commonly chosen. As the patient may not be allowed to eat certain foods, flowers are the safest bet. However, pot plants (**はちうえの花**) are not considered appropriate for a sick person in Japan, because they imply a long illness. Certain flowers such as camellias (**つばき**) are considered unlucky because the blossom falls off in one piece, like a severed head. Chrysanthemums (**きく**) should not be chosen, either, because they are considered to be flowers for funerals.

| はちうえの花 | つばき | きく |

If you are going to visit a close friend, you may also take something s/he is fond of, such as a music tape or a book. ⇨CN S-2

172

c. Expressions of encouragement

The following expressions will be much appreciated: ⇨CN S-4

① **お元気そうですね。**　　　　*You look well.*

② **顔色がよくて、安心しました。**　*I feel relieved because you're a good colour.*

③ **大丈夫ですよ。**　　　　　*You'll be fine.*

④ **すぐに元気になりますよ。**　　*You'll recover soon.*

When you are leaving, use 「**じゃ、そろそろ失礼します。**（*Well, I have to go now.*）」 followed by 「**どうぞお大事に。**（*Hope you get well soon.*）」

2. Condolences and celebration

a. Condolences（**お悔やみ**）

When a member of someone's family has died, you express your sympathy with the expressions below; they are very formal and the part in（　）is often abbreviated or just mumbled:

① **このたびは、どうも（ごしゅうしょうさまでした）。**

Please accept my sympathy (for your bereavement).

② **お母さまがおなくなりになったと伺って、びっくりいたしました。**

It was a terrible shock to hear about your mother's death.

③ **どうかあまりお力をおとされないように。**

Please don't be too dejected.

④ **何か私にできることがありましたら、どうぞ何でもおっしゃってください。**

If there's anything I can do, please feel free to ask me.

b. Celebration (お祝い)

On a happy occasion you can offer your congratulations by using the following expressions:

① **このたびは、本当におめでとうございます／ました。**

Congratulations on this happy occasion.

②

ご結婚 ご入学 ご卒業 ご出産 お誕生日	**おめでとうございます。** *Congratulations on*	*your marriage.* *your entering school.* *your graduation.* *the birth of your baby.* *your birthday.*

＜Strategies＞

S-1. How to start a conversation —9. Visiting a sick person

As we saw in L8, when you enter a room, you knock first and then say 失礼します. The patient may greet you with これはどうも *Thank you for coming*.

The next step is to enquire about the patient's condition:「具合いはいかがですか。 *How are you feeling?*.」

After getting a reply about the patient's condition, you normally express your sympathy with 「大変でしたね。 *You've had a hard time.*」.

Look at the following exchanges:

① ▣A ：（Knock-knock）失礼します。

　　B ：ああ、これはどうも。

　　A ：具合いはいかがですか。

　　B ：ええ、まあ、何とか。

　　A ：大変でしたね。

② ⒼA ：（Knock-knock）失礼します。

　　B ：やあ、こりゃどうも。 ♟

　　A ：どう↗、具合いは。

　　B ：うん、ちょっと胃をやられちゃってね。
　　　　 Hmm, my stomach has been damaged a bit.

　　A ：大変だったわね。 ♟

S-2. How to give a present

a. When giving a present to a sick person, you don't use つまらないものですが (⇨ L19CN S-2). Instead, 「これ、お見舞いなんですけど。」or「あのう、これ...（handing over the present）」are often used. If you are not close to the sick person, you need not say much when giving your present. The receiver will usually not express any hesitation in this situation, and accept with「ご心配いただいて、おそれいります。（*Thank*

175

you for your kindness. 」, 「ご心配いただいて、ありがとうございます。」 or 「どうも（ありがとう）。」.

①A：あの、これ、どうぞ。

B：ああ、ご心配いただいて、おそれいります。

②学生：先生、これ、お見舞いなんですけど。

先生：ああ、これはどうも。

③先生：Bさん、これ、お見舞い。

学生：あ、どうもありがとうございます。

④A：はい、これ。

B：わあ、ありがとう。

b. If you have chosen a personalized gift, you might add your reasons for choosing it:

①A：あの、これ、音楽テープなんですけど。

B：あ、これはどうも。

A：たいくつなさってるんじゃないかと思って。
  I thought you might be bored.

B：どうもありがとう。

②A：あ、これ、インドのおかし。

B：えっ、ほんと。↗

A：なつかしいんじゃないかと思って。
  I thought you might have a craving for them.

B：わあ。何よりのお見舞いだよ。
  Wow—that's the most wonderful gift!
  どうもありがとう。

③A：あの、これ、お見舞い。

　　B：わあ、何かしら。

　　A：まんがの本なんだ。　　　　　　*It's a comic book.*

　　B：ありがとう。ちょうどたいくつしてたの。
　　　Thanks. Just in time—I was bored.

S-3. How to ask about the patient's condition:
symptoms, progress, how long it will take, etc.

　　If the sick person is permitted to talk, you can ask about details like the symptoms, how it happened, how things are going, and how long it'll take to get better.

a. Two ways of asking about the patient's condition

　　You can ask directly with expressions like 「**いかがですか／どうですか、どう**↗。 *How are you?*」,「**どんな具合いですか**。 *How are you feeling?*」 or 「**どうなさったんですか／どうしたんですか**。 *What happened to you?*」.

①A：どうなさったんですか。

　　B：ええ、盲腸の手術をしたんですよ。
　　　Well, I had my appendix taken out.

　　A：盲腸ですか。大変でしたね。

②A：どう↗、具合いは。

　　B：うん、スキーで足の骨、折っちゃって。

　　A：スキーで。

　　B：まあ、たいしたことはないんだけどね。
　　　Well, it's not serious at all.

　　You can also begin the conversation by indicating what you heard from others; if you heard that the patient has a stomach trouble, for instance, you might ask **〜んですって**。↗（♀） or **〜だそうですね**。. If someone told you that it was a bicycle accident, you can ask 「**自転車に乗ってたんですって**。↗」. The patient will thus be prompted to correct your information if wrong, and continue the story about what happened if right:

第 二十二 課

③ 🔲A：胃が悪いんですって。↗

B：いえ、胃じゃなくて肝臓なんです。
No, it's not the stomach but the liver.

A：肝臓

B：ええ。ちょっと酒を飲みすぎちゃってね。

A：そうですか。

④ 😊A：自転車に乗ってたんだって。↗

B：うん。交差点で車にぶつけられちゃって。
Yeah, I was hit by a car at an intersection.

A：ええっ、あぶないなあ。👕

B：いや、向こうが悪いんだよ。👕

⑤ 😊A：スキーで足の骨、折ったんだって。↗

B：うん。うしろから来た人にぶつけられちゃって。

A：まあ、あぶないわね。👧

B：あら、向こうが悪いのよ。👧

b. Asking how long it'll take

Having enquired about the patient's condition, you can ask how long it will take to be discharged:

① 🔲A：長くかかるんですか。 *Will you be here for a long time?*

B：いえ、あと 2 週間ぐらいで出られるんですよ。

A：そうですか。

② 😊A：いつごろ退院できるの。↗

B：あと 1 週間ぐらいかしら。👧

A：そう。↘

③ 😊A：いつごろ退院できるんだい。↗ 👕

B：あと 1 週間ぐらいかな。

A：そう。↘

178

S-4. How to cheer up the patient

If you find out that the patient's condition or injury is not so serious, you can say things to cheer up（元気づける）the patient:

①📺心配しなくても、大丈夫ですよ。

　心配いりませんよ。　　　　　　　　　　　　*No need to worry.*

②📺すぐに元気になりますよ。　　　　　　　　*You'll be OK soon.*

③🈁元気を出して。　　　　　　　　　　　　　*Brace yourself.*

④📺A：どんな具合いですか。

　　B：いや、たいしたことないんですよ。　　*It's not serious.*

　　　　医者は1週間って言ってるんです。

　　A：そうですか。じゃ、もう少しのしんぼうですね。
　　　　I see. Not much longer to go, then.

⑤🈁A：どのくらいかかるの。↗

　　B：それが1ケ月ぐらいかかりそうなの。♀

　　A：そう。↘　でも、まあ、単純骨折なら、心配いらないよ。♂

　　B：ええ。

　　A：がんばって、一日も早くよくなれよ。♂
　　　　Try your best to get better as soon as possible.

Sometimes words of encouragement（はげまし）are useful not only for a sick person but also for a depressed person:

⑥📺A：どうしたんですか。

　　B：実は、2週間も家族から手紙が来ないんですよ。

　　A：そうですか。でも、まあ、知らせがないのはよい知らせって言いますからね。
　　　　Well, but people say that no news is good news.

　　B：ええ。

　　A：元気を出してください。

CN

However, when it is serious, or when the patient is a senior, you don't say much—just listen attentively to the patient's explanation, with some Aizuchi to show your sympathy.

When leaving, the following can be used:

⑦🈁どうぞお大事_{だいじ}に。 *Please take care.*

⑧🈁はやく元気_{げんき}になってください。 *Please get well soon.*

S-5. Asking someone to be more careful

If the patient has done/is doing something dangerous, you can use the following expressions to tell him to be more careful:

気_きを { つけてくださいね。🈁 *Please be careful.*
つけてね。🅖♦
つけろよ。🅖♦

注意_{ちゅうい} { してくださいね。🈁
してね。🅖♦
しろよ。🅖♦

You can also use the direct request forms, 〜てください／〜ないでください, adding the reason why s/he ought to be more careful:

①🈁A：気をつけてくださいね。自転車_{じてんしゃ}はあぶないですから。

B：はい。

②🈁A：忘_{わす}れないでくださいね。あしたは大事_{だいじ}な会議_{かいぎ}ですから。

B：ええ。

③🅖A：落_おとさないでね。大切_{たいせつ}なものが入_{はい}ってるから。♦

B：うん。

④🅖A：注意しろよ。タバコのすいすぎは体_{からだ}によくないから。♦

B：わかってるわよ。♦

第23課

頼みと断わり
たの　　こと
Making and refusing a request

OBJECTIVES:

Model Conversation

Characters : Suzuki(鈴木), Anil Sharma(アニル・シャルマ), Yamashita(山下)

Situation : Suzuki-san asks Anil-san to help him with his work, but Anil-san refuses. Suzuki-san then persuades Yamashita-san to help him.

Flow-chart :

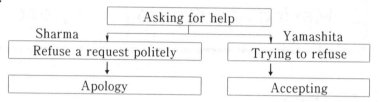

―研究室で―

鈴　木　：アニルさん、いる。
シャルマ：はい。
鈴　木　：あ、よかった。いま、ちょっといいかな。
シャルマ：はい。何でしょうか。
鈴　木　：実は、いまうちの研究室で、
シャルマ：ええ。
鈴　木　：センターの方からソフト頼まれてるんだけど。
シャルマ：ええ。
鈴　木　：アニルさん、BASIC わかるよね。
シャルマ：ええ、だいたいわかると思いますけど。
鈴　木　：じゃ、すまないけど、ちょっと手伝ってもらえないかな。

　　　　　＊　　　　＊　　　　＊

シャルマ：あの、それ、急ぎますか。
鈴　木　：うん。今週中にセンターの方に渡すことになってるから。
シャルマ：あの、実は、今週中に書かなくちゃならないレポートがあるんです。
鈴　木　：そうか。じゃ、ちょっと無理だな。
シャルマ：ええ。来週なら時間があるんですけど。
鈴　木　：じゃ、山下にでも頼んでみるかな。
シャルマ：すみません、お役に立てなくて。
鈴　木　：いや、いいんだよ。じゃ、また。
シャルマ：どうもすみませんでした。

―ろうかで―

鈴　木：お、山下。
山　下：あ、どうも。
鈴　木：レポート、もう終わった。
山　下：ええ。いま出してきたところなんですけど。
鈴　木：あ、ちょうどよかった。
山　下：あの、何か。
鈴　木：いや、あの、例のソフトなんだけどさ。
山　下：ああ、あれ。たしか、今週中でしたね。
鈴　木：そうなんだよ。悪いんだけど、ちょっと手伝ってくれないかな。

　　　　　　＊　　　＊　　　＊

山　下：いまからですか。
鈴　木：うん。
山　下：きのう、レポートで徹夜だったんですよ。
鈴　木：そこを何とか頼むよ。
山　下：ちょっと……。

　　　　　　＊　　　＊　　　＊

鈴　木：いや、おれ一人じゃ間に合いそうもなくてさ。な。
山　下：まいったな。
鈴　木：悪いな。晩めし、おごるからさ。
山　下：はい。やります。
鈴　木：いや、悪い、悪い。

MC

Report

<鈴木さんの日記>

　日本語教育のためのコンピュータ・プログラムを作らなければならないので、とても忙しい。今週中に留学生センターに渡すことになっているが、一人では間に合いそうもない。それで，だれかに手伝ってもらうことにした。

　アニルさんに頼んでみたが、レポートで忙しくて無理だった。困っていたら、たまたま山下君に会った。ちょうどレポートを出してきたところで、ゆうべは徹夜だったそうだ。でも、あと2日しかないので無理に頼んだ。彼ならちゃんとやってくれるだろう。

New Words and Expressions

Words in the conversation

頼み	たのみ	making a request
断わり	ことわり	refusing a request, declining an offer
センター		(International Student) Center
～の方	～のほう	the side of ～, in the direction of ～
～用	～よう	for the use of～
ソフト		software
BASIC	ベーシック	a computer language
だいたい		more or less
急ぐ	いそぐ	to hurry
今週中に	こんしゅうちゅうに	within this week
渡す	わたす	to hand over, to give
ろうか		corridor
例の～	れいの～	you know that ～
徹夜	てつや	(sitting up) all night
何とか	なんとか	somehow
おれ		I 🄲 ♠
まいる		to be beaten, to give in
晩めし	ばんめし	dinner 🄲 ♠
おごる		to treat

＜Expressions in the conversation＞

よかった。　　　　　　　　　　*Thank god.*

You can say this when something has gone well.

BASIC わかるよね。↗　　　　*You understand BASIC, don't you?* 🄲

よね is used to ask for confirmation about something that may be clear to the listener.

すまないけど、～　　　　　　*Excuse me, but ～* 🄲 ⇨CN S-2a

In formal speech, **すみませんが** is used. ⇨L4CN S-1

渡すことになってる　　　　　*I'm supposed to hand it over.*

～ことになっている shows that some matter has been decided. ⇨GNⅢ

書かなくちゃならない   *I have to write.*
か

    ～なくてはならない *must* ～ often becomes ～なくちゃならない in casual
speech. ⇨GN I

すみません、お役に立てなくて。   *Sorry I'm no help.* ⇨CN S-3c
        やく た

いま出してきたところなんですけど。   *I just handed it in.*
   だ

    ～たところ shows that something has just been done. ⇨GN IV
    ところ is often pronounced as とこ in casual speech.

ちょうどよかった。   *(You came at) just the right time.*

    You can say this when something has happened at just the right time.

悪いんだけど、～   *Sorry, but* ～ ⇨CN S-2a
わる

そこを何とか頼むよ。   *Please do me a favour.* ⇨CN S-5
    なん たの

ちょっと……。   *I'm afraid I can't help you.* ⇨CN S-3a

間に合いそうもなくてさ。   *It doesn't look as though I'll make it.*
ま あ

    ～そうもない is used when something is unlikely to happen. ⇨L17GN III
    ～て（explaining the circumstances）is often used for making an excuse.
    ⇨CN S-5
    さ is added for getting the listener's attention in casual speech.

な。↗   *You know?*

まいったな。   *I'm beaten.*

    困ったな is used in a similar situation by both men and women.
    こま

悪いな。   *Sorry.*
わる

晩めし、おごるからさ。   *I'll treat you to dinner.*
ばん

    ～から（implying that you will do something in return）is useful for
persuading someone. ⇨CN S-5

Words in the report

日本語教育	にほんごきょういく	*Japanese language teaching*
コンピュータ・プログラム		*computer programme*
たまたま		*by chance, accidentally*
ゆうべ		*last night*
無理に	むりに	*forcedly*

<Expressions in the report>

作らなければならない。　　　　　　　　*I have to write* (a computer programme).
　　　　〜なければならない ⇨GN I

手伝ってもらうことにした。　　　　　　*I decided to get help.*
　　　　〜ことにする ⇨GN III

＊NOTE＊　＜period of time＞ 中 differs from ＜action＞ 中. ⇨L15GN VIII
　　　〜中 indicates that something continues over a period of time:

　　　　① 午前中ずっと頭が痛かった。

　　　　② きょうは、一日中テレビを見ていた。

　〜中に indicates that something happens within a certain period of time.

　　　　① 午前中に母から電話があった。

　　　　② 今日中にレポートを書いてしまおう。

The use of 中 can be read in three ways:
　　　1）〈action〉－ちゅう　　　：電話中、会議中、工事中、etc.
　　　2）〈place〉－じゅう　　　：日本中、世界中、大学中、etc.
　　　3）〈period〉－じゅう　　　：一日中、一晩中、一年中、今日中、etc.
　　　　　　－ちゅう　　　　：午前中、夏休み中、etc.
　　　　　　－ちゅう／じゅう：今週中、今月中、etc.

MC

Grammar Notes

Ⅰ.　〜なければならない ｝ *must 〜／ have to 〜／ should 〜*
　　〜なくてはいけない ｝： *ought to 〜*

Examples

① 今週中にレポートを書かなければなりません。
　こんしゅうちゅう　　　　　　　　　か
(I) have to write a report by the end of this week.

② 薬を飲まなくてはいけませんよ。
　くすり　の
(You) must take the medicine.

③ もっと強くなければ。
　　　　つよ
(You) must become stronger.

【*Explanation*】

Combining 〜なければ／〜なくては with ならない／いけない results in the meaning of *must 〜* or *have to 〜*（*lit. if (you) don't 〜, it won't do*）; 書かなければならない, 書かなくてはならない, 書かなければいけない and 書かなくてはいけない all mean *have to write ／ must write*.

　〜なければ／〜なくては can be derived by replacing the final **-i** of the **-nai** form with ければ or くては:

書かない		書かなければ／書かなくては
食べない		食べなければ／食べなくては
た	┌ければ	
安くない	‥‥‥‥	安くなければ／安くなくては
やす	└くては →	
便利じゃない		便利じゃなければ／便利じゃなくては
べんり		
東京じゃない		東京じゃなければ／東京じゃなくては
とうきょう		

Then add ならない or いけない:

〜なければ（なけりゃ）／（なきゃ） ＋	ならない（なんない）
〜なくては（なくちゃ）	いけない

↓

書かなければならない
書かなくてはならない　　　*(I) have to write (something).*
書かなければいけない
書かなくてはいけない

The expressions in brackets（**なけりゃ，なきゃ** etc.）are shortened forms which are often used in casual speech. **ならない** and **いけない** are also often omitted in casual speech:

1. レポートを書かなきゃ。　　*(I) have to write a report.*

2. 今すぐ行かなくちゃ。　　*(I) have to go straightaway.*

3. お金を払わなけりゃ。　　*(I) have to pay.*

4. きれいじゃなくちゃ。　　*(It) has to be clean.*

Verb forms [V-nai] [V-nakute] & [V-nakereba]				
	Dic. form	[V-nai]	[V-nakute]	[V-nakereba]
Group I	iku　*to go* 行く	ikanai 行かない	ikanakute 行かなくて	ikanakereba 行かなければ
	nomu　*to drink* 飲む	nomanai 飲まない	nomanakute 飲まなくて	nomanakereba 飲まなければ
	toru　*to take* とる	toranai とらない	toranakute とらなくて	toranakereba とらなければ
	matsu　*to wait* 待つ	matanai 待たない	matanakute 待たなくて	matanakereba 待たなければ
	iu　*to say* 言う	iwanai 言わない	iwanakute 言わなくて	iwanakereba 言わなければ
	au　*to meet* 会う	awanai 会わない	awanakute 会わなくて	awanakereba 会わなければ
	hanasu *to speak* 話す	hanasanai 話さない	hanasanakute 話さなくて	hanasanakereba 話さなければ

GN

Group II	taberu *to eat* 食べる	tabenai 食べない	tabenakute 食べなくて	tabenakereba 食べなければ
	miru *to see* 見る	minai 見ない	minakute 見なくて	minakereba 見なければ
	okiru *to wake up* 起きる	okinai 起きない	okinakute 起きなくて	okinakereba 起きなければ
Group III	kuru *to come* 来る	konai 来ない	konakute 来なくて	konakereba 来なければ
	suru *to do* する	shinai しない	shinakute しなくて	shinakereba しなければ
	benkyoo suru *to study* 勉強する	benkyoo shinai 勉強しない	benkyoo shinakute 勉強しなくて	benkyoo shinakereba 勉強しなければ

[**V-nakute**] is one of the two negative **-te** forms: recall the other one, [**V-naide**]. ⇨L8GNⅢ

Ⅱ. 〜なくてもいい: *(You) needn't 〜*

The opposite of 〜なければならない／〜なくてはいけない is 〜なくてもいい *(lit. even if (you) don't 〜, it will be OK)*, which means *you don't have to 〜* or *you needn't 〜*.

> [**V-nakute**] もいいです

1. あしたは日曜日（にちようび）ですから、研究室（けんきゅうしつ）に行（い）かなくてもいいです。
   Tomorrow is Sunday, so I don't have to go to the Lab tomorrow.

2. A：いくらですか。　　　*How much is it?*

   B：払（はら）わなくてもいいです。ただですから。
   No need to pay for it. It's free.

3. A：薬を飲まなければいけませんか。
　　　　くすり　の
   Do I have to take medicine?

   B：いいえ、飲まなくてもいいですよ。
   No, you don't have to.

Ⅲ. ～ことにする: *decide to ～*
　　～ことになる: *～ be decided / arranged*　する verbs and なる verbs〈6〉

Examples

①　A：これから飲みに行こう。
　　　　　　　　　　い
　　　Let's go for a drink.

　　B：いや、残念だな。今から木村先生と会うことになっているんだ。
　　　　　　　ざんねん　　　いま　きむらせんせい　あ
　　　*Oh, what a pity. I have to meet Kimura-sensee. (lit. It's been arranged that I
　　　am to meet Kimura-sensee now.)*

②　留学生はセンターで6か月日本語を勉強することになっています。
　　りゅうがくせい　　　　　　げつにほんご　べんきょう
　　*Foreign students have to study Japanese for 6 months at the (International
　　Student) Center. (lit. It's been decided that foreign students will study Japanese
　　for 6 months at the (International Student) Center.)*

③　A：夏休みはどうするの。
　　　　なつやす
　　　What are you going to do during the summer vacation?

　　B：北海道に行くことにしたよ。
　　　　ほっかいどう
　　　I've decided to go to Hokkaido.

【*Explanation*】

　　　[V-(r)u] ことにする means *to decide to do*, whereas [V-(r)u] ことになる means
to be decided, to come about. Recall that こと *fact/matter* has the function of nominalizing
a sentence. ⇨L18GNⅢ

　　As we saw in earlier lessons（L3, L9, L21）, する verbs imply the existence of
an actor responsible for the action of the verb, whereas なる verbs describe actions
where the actor is unknown or where a change of state comes about naturally. With this
in mind, consider the following examples.

GN

IV. 〜ところだ(ところ〈2〉): *be just about to 〜, be just 〜 ing, have just 〜*

Examples

① A：勉強しろよ。
   べんきょう
   Do your work.

   B：今するところだよ。
     いま
   I am just about to.

② 手紙を書いているところです。
   てがみ か
   I'm just writing a letter.

③ レポートを出してきたところです。
         だ
   I've just submitted my report.

【*Explanation*】

ところ means literally *place* or *point in time/moment*. Depending on the form of the verb preceeding it, ところ can be used to describe matters/events which are just about to happen, are just happening, or have just happened: ⇨L12GNⅧ

[V (plain)]		
[V-(r)u] 洗濯する <small>せんたく</small>	ところだ	〈*just about to ～*〉 　洗濯するところだ。 　*I'm just about to do the laundry.*
[V-te] いる 洗濯している		〈*just doing ～*〉 　洗濯しているところだ。 　*I'm just doing the laundry.*
[V-ta] 洗濯した		〈*have just done something ～*〉 　洗濯したところだ。 　*I've just done the laundry.*

するところ　　　　　しているところ　　　　　したところ

V．〜ため: *for (the purpose of) ～, for (the benefit of) ～*

Examples
---

① 日本へ留学するために日本語を勉強しています。
<small>にほん　りゅうがく　　　　　にほんご　べんきょう</small>
I'm studying Japanese for the purpose of going to Japan to study.

② 日本へ留学するための書類をなくしました。
<small>しょるい</small>
I've lost the documents for going to Japan to study.

③ 入学試験のために夜遅くまで勉強しています。
<small>にゅうがくしけん　　　　よるおそ　　　勉強</small>
I'm studying until late at night for the entrance exams.

④ 入学試験のための準備が大変です。
<small>じゅんび　たいへん</small>
The preparation for the entrance exams is very hard.

GN

⑤ 先生のためにプレゼントを買いましょう。
Let's buy a present for the teacher.

⑥ 先生のためのプレゼントはどれですか。
Which one's the present for the teacher?

【*Explanation*】

1. The meaning of ため

Used after [V-(r)u] or [N] の, 〜ため indicates purpose; when the noun of [N] の is a person or country etc., 〜ため indicates benefit.

[V-(r)u] ため

1. 日本へ留学するため　*for (the purpose of) going Japan to study*

[N] のため

2. 入学試験のため　　*for (the purpose of) the entrance examination*

3. 先生のため　　　　*for (the benefit of) the teacher*

4. 国のため　　　　　*for (my) country*

2. ための vs ために

The thing or action that serves to fulfil the purpose, etc., comes after **ため**. Note that when it is a thing that serves the purpose or benefits the beneficiary (i.e. when **ため** modifies another noun), **ための** is used, but when it is an action that helps to achieve the purpose (i.e. when **ため** modifies a verb) **ために** is used.

1.　　　　〈purpose〉　　　　〈the action which achieves the purpose〉
[日本へ留学する　ため　に]　　日本語を　勉強しています。

I'm studying Japanese for the purpose of going to Japan to study.

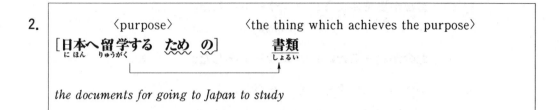

2.

　　　　　〈purpose〉　　　　　　〈the thing which achieves the purpose〉

［日本へ留学する　ため　の］　　　書類
　にほん　りゅうがく　　　　　　　　　　しょるい

the documents for going to Japan to study

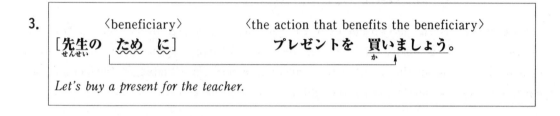

3.

　　　　〈beneficiary〉　　　　〈the action that benefits the beneficiary〉

［先生の　ため　に］　　　　　プレゼントを　買いましょう。
　せんせい　　　　　　　　　　　　　　　　　　　か

Let's buy a present for the teacher.

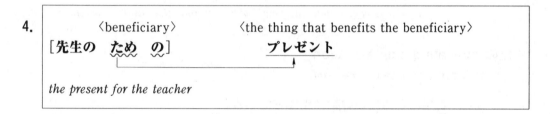

4.

　　　　〈beneficiary〉　　　　〈the thing that benefits the beneficiary〉

［先生の　ため　の］　　　　　プレゼント
　せんせい

the present for the teacher

3. The difference between ように and ために

Recall the following sentence from Lesson 21:

1. 忘れないようにノートに書いた。
　わす　　　　　　　　　　か
　I wrote it in my notebook so that I wouldn't forget it.

Although both **ように** and **ために** indicate purpose, they are used with different types of verbs:

| [するV] ために | [なるV] ように |
| | [V-nai] |

ために is attached to **する** verbs (which can be controlled by the actor's will), whereas **ように** is attached to **なる** verbs, including potential forms and negative forms, which cannot be controlled by the actor's will). Look at the following examples:

2. ○　お金を集めるためにコンサートをした。
　　　かね　あつ
　　We held a concert for the purpose of collecting money.

×　お金を集めるようにコンサートをした。

195

3. ○ お金が集まるようにコンサートをした。
   We held a concert so that money would come in.

   × お金が集まるためにコンサートをした。

4. ○ 雨にぬれないようにかさをさした。
   I opened the umbrella so that I wouldn't get wet.

   × 雨にぬれないためにかさをさした。

However, when the two halves of the sentence have different subjects, ように can be used with する verbs, too. This is because the actor of the main clause cannot control the actions of the actor of the embedded clause. In example 5., the person who cut the vegetables cannot control the children's eating them.

5. ○ 子供がやさいをよく食べるように小さく切った。
   I cut the vegetables into small pieces so that the children would eat lots.

4. ため indicating cause/reason

~ため can also mean *because (of)* ~:

1. 台風のために新幹線は止まっている。
   Because of the typhoon, the Shinkansen has stopped running.

2. 先生が病気のために授業は休みだ。
   Because our teacher is ill (lit. Because of the illness of our teacher), the class is cancelled.

3. 部屋に友だちが来たために宿題ができなかった。
   Because a/my friend came to my room, I couldn't do my homework.

The difference between the two uses of ため depends on the form of the verb to which ため is attached; after non-past positive verb forms（[V-(r)u] ため, ex. 留学するため）the meaning is *purpose*, but after past verb forms（[V-ta] ため, ex. 留学したため）ため can only express *reason*.

196

Conversation Notes

＜*General Information*＞

1. Expressions of apology

You can apologize with varying degrees of formality:

申しわけございません。▣▮	申しわけない。 ©⬇⬅🚹
申しわけありません。▣▮	すまない。／すまん。©⬇⬅🚹
すみません。 ▣	ごめんなさい。 ©⬇⬅👤
	ごめん。／悪い。 ©⬇⬅

You can add **どうも** to the formal expressions above.

When you apologize for something that has already been done before, use the past form of each expression except for **ごめんなさい／ごめん**.

Look at the examples below dealing with a variety of situations.

a. Apologizing for one's fault/mistake ⇨L13CN S-1, L21CN S-4

① **遅くなって、ごめん。**
Sorry to be late.

② **すみません。うっかりして。**
Sorry I was so careless.

③ **気がつかなくて、申しわけありません。**
I'm sorry I didn't notice it.

b. Apologizing for giving someone trouble ⇨L15CN S-4

① **おじゃまして、すみませんでした。**
I'm sorry to have disturbed you.

② **すみません、お手数かけて。**
Sorry to trouble you. (Thank you for your help.)

③ **ごめいわくかけて、申しわけありませんでした。**
I'm sorry to have troubled you.

c. Apologizing for declining an offer ⇨L17CN S-3

悪いけど   ⬇ ┃ ちょっと……。
すみませんが、⬆⬅ ┃

I'm sorry but...

d. Apologizing for refusing a request ⇨L23CN S-3

すみません。お役に立てなくて。

Sorry I'm no help.

<Strategies>

S-1. How to start a conversation —10. Making a request

a. When asking someone to do something for you, you can mention what your problem is: ⇨L5CN S-1

〈problem〉ん | ですけど。🈁
　　　　　　| だけど。　🈀

① あの、いま、日本語でレポート書いてるんですけど。
　　　　　　にほんご　　　　　　　　か
I'm writing a report in Japanese now.

If the listener knows about your problem, you can begin with 例の [N]:
　　　　　　　　　　　　　　　　　　　　　　　　　　れい

例の [N] なん | ですけど。🈁
れい　　　　　| だけど。　🈀

② あの、例のソフトなんだけどさ。
It's the software that you've heard about.

b. After that, you can ask for the necessary information:

1) Asking if the listener has enough time

〈time〉 | お時間ございますか。🈁🔼　*Do you have time 〜 ?*
　　　　|　じかん
　　　　| 時間ありますか。　　　🈁
　　　　| 時間ある。↗　　　　　🈀

① きょうの午後、お時間ございますか。
　　　　　　ごご　　じかん
Do you have time this afternoon?

2) Asking if the listener can do it. ⇨L20CN S-3b

[N] | おわかりになりますか。🈁🔼　*Do you understand 〜 ?*
　　| わかりますか。　　　　🈁
　　| わかる。↗　　　　　　🈀

[N] | お使いになったことありますか。🈁🔼　*Have you used 〜 before?*
　　| つか
　　| 使ったことありますか。　　　🈁
　　| 使ったことある。↗　　　　　🈀

199

② **BASIC、わかるよね。** ↗

You understand BASIC, don't you?

③ **このソフト、使ったことありますか。**

Have you used this software before?

S-2. How to make a request

a. You can introduce a request politely as follows:

申しわけありませんが、 🗾⬆   *Excuse me but,*
すみませんが、 🗾
すまないけど、 🙂⬇🕴
悪いけど、 🙂

Or you can say more eagerly as follows:

申しわけないんですが、 🗾⬆
悪いんだけど、 🙂

b. Then you can go on to make your request: ⇨L14GN Ⅱ，L20CN S-3a

1) Using the potential form of [V-te] もらう／[V-te] いただく

[V-te] | **いただけませんか。** 🗾⬆   *Could you please ～ ?*
      | **もらえませんか。** 🗾   */Would you mind ～ ?*
      | **もらえない。** ↗ 🙂

① **すみませんが、ワープロの使い方を教えてくださいませんか。**

Could you please teach me how to use a word processor?

2) Using [V-te] くれる／[V-te] くださる

[V-te] | **くださいませんか。** 🗾⬆   *Could you please ～ ?*
      | **くれませんか。** 🗾   */Would you mind ～ ?*
      | **くれない。** ↗ 🙂

② **悪いけど、ちょっとお金貸してくれない。**

Could you lend me some money?

If you want to be more polite, you can add **でしょうか** or **かな**.

③ **あの、申しわけありませんが、ちょっと日本語をチェックしていただけないでしょうか。**
Excuse me but would you mind if I ask you to check my Japanese for me?

④ **すまないけど、ちょっと手伝ってもらえないかな。**
Would you mind helping me, please?

c. You can also make a request with **たい** or **ほしい**:

1) Using [V-te] **もらいたい**／[V-te] **いただきたい**

[V-te] | **いただきたいんですが。** 🈁🈂　*Could you please ～?*
　　　| **もらいたいんですが。**　🈁　*/Would you mind ～?*
　　　| **もらいたいんだけど。**　☻

① **あの、ちょっと日本語をチェックしていただきたいんですが。**
Excuse me. Would you mind checking my Japanese for me?

② **ちょっと翻訳の仕事を手伝ってもらいたいんだけど。**
Could you please help me with my translation?

2) Using [V-te] **ほしい**　⇨L17GNⅡ

[V-te] | **ほしいんですが。** 🈁　　*I'd like you ～.*
　　　| **ほしいんだけど。** ☻

③ **ちょっと切手買ってきてほしいんだけど。**
I'd like you to buy some stamps for me.

S-3. How to refuse a request politely

a. When you have been asked to do something, you can refuse the request immediately but politely with **ちょっと**: ⇨L17CN S-3

申しわけありませんが、　|　**ちょっと……。**　*I'm sorry but I...*
すみませんが、　　　　　|　　　　　　　　　*(I can't help you.)*
悪いけど、

201

You can ask how urgent the request is before deciding to refuse it:

お急ぎでしょうか。 🔲🔼   *Are you in a hurry?*
急ぎますか。   🔲
急ぐの。 ↗   🔘

先生：すまないけど、英語のチェックをしてくれないかな。
　せんせい　　　　　えいご
　　Would you mind checking my English for me?

学生：あの、それ、お急ぎでしょうか。
　がくせい
　　Are you in a hurry?

先生：うん。あしたまでなんだ。
　　Yes, (I need it done) by tomorrow.

学生：そうですか。すみませんが、じつはちょっと……。
　　I'm sorry but...

b. You can also give a reason why you are unable to accept the request.
⇨L18CN S-3a

〈reason〉│ んです。 🔲
　　　　　│ んだ。　 🔘
　　　　　│ の。　　 🔘👤

① すみませんが、今週 中に書かなくちゃならないレポートがあるんで
　　　　　　　　こんしゅうちゅう　か
　す。
　I have a report I must finish this week.

② 悪いけど、いまちょっと時間がないんだ。
　わる　　　　　　　　　　じかん
　I'm sorry but I don't have time now.

Or you may also wish to offer an alternative:

[N] なら、～│ んですけど。 🔲
　　　　　　│ んだけど。　 🔘

① 来週なら、お手伝いできるんですけど。
　らいしゅう　てつだ
　I can help you next week.

② 中国語なら、わかるんだけど。
　ちゅうごくご
　If it were Chinese I'd understand.

c. When you've refused a request, you can end the conversation with an apology by using **お役に立てなくて** in formal speech.

お役に立てなくて、 ｜ 申しわけありません。📷⬆
　　　　　　　　　　｜ すみません。　　　　📷

Sorry I'm no help.

You can also use the following expressions:

申しわけありません。｜ お役に立てなくて。
すみません。　　　　｜

S-4. How to withdraw a request that is refused

When you get a negative reaction to your request, you can withdraw it by way of an apology, in formal speech:

① （A、B：not intimate）

📷A：すみませんが、ちょっと……。

　B：あ、そうですか。どうもすみませんでした。
　　　I see. I'm sorry to have bothered you.

②📷先生：悪いけど、いま、ちょっと忙しいんだ。
　　　　　Sorry but I'm busy now.

　学生：あ、そうですか。　　　　*Oh, I see.*

　先生：悪いね。　　　　　　　　*Sorry.*

　学生：いいえ、どうもおじゃましました。
　　　　Not at all. I'm sorry to have bothered you.

In casual speech, you can withdraw your request as follows:

③ （A🔺、B🔻：友だち）

　A：悪いけど、ちょっと……。　　*I'm afraid I...*

　B：あ、そう。　　　　　　　　　*I see.*

　A：ごめんね。　　　　　　　　　*Sorry.*

　B：いや、いいんだ。　　　　　　*It's O.K.*

203

S-5. How to persuade someone to accept your request

Even if your request was refused once, you can try again with **そこを何^{なん}とか**:

そこを何とか	お願^{ねが}いできないでしょうか。🈯（polite）
	お願いできませんか。　　　　🈯
	お願いします。　　　　　　　🈯
	お願い。　　　　　　　　　　☺♀
	頼^{たの}む。　　　　　　　　　　☺♂
	……。　　　　　　　　　　🈯／☺

Could you please...?

If necessary, you can mention why you need help, or bargain for help:

1) Making an excuse

   ① 一人^{ひとり}で困^{こま}ってるんです。
     It's difficult all by myself.

   ② ほかに頼める人^{ひと}がいなくて。
     I don't have anyone else I can ask.

   ③ おれ一人じゃ、間^まに合^あいそうもなくてさ。☺♂
     It doesn't look like I'll be able to finish it by myself.

2) Bargaining

   ④ 30分^{ぷん}でいいですから。
     Only for 30 minutes.

   ⑤ 晩^{ばん}めし、おごるからさ。☺♂
     I'll treat you to dinner.

If you have succeeded in persuading the listener to help you, you can finish the conversation with an expression of thanks involving **助^{たす}かります** *I appreciate your help*:

どうもすみません。助かります。🈯　　*Thank you for your help.*
悪^{わる}いね。助かるよ。　　　　　☺♂
悪いわね。助かるわ。　　　　　　☺♀

第24課

旅行の相談
りょこう　　そうだん
Planning a trip

OBJECTIVES:

GRAMMAR

- Ⅰ. ～(の)なら〈2〉: *if it is the case ～/if ～*
- Ⅱ. ～ても: *even if ～*
- Ⅲ. ～のに: *despite ～/although ～*
- Ⅳ. ～はずだ: *supposed to ～/should ～/ought to ～*
- Ⅴ. ～わけだ: *That's why ～/No wonder ～*
- Ⅵ. 実は、やっぱり、せっかく: sentence adverbs
  じつ

CONVERSATION

＜General Information＞
1. Useful information for planning a trip
2. Japanese inns

＜Strategies＞
S-1. How to make a proposal
S-2. How to voice disagreement
S-3. How to support someone's view
S-4. How to ask for someone's approval
S-5. How to avoid a definite statement

205

Model Conversation

Characters：Yamashita(山下), Tanaka(田中), Suzuki(鈴木)

Situation：Yamashita-san invites Tanaka-san and Lisa-san to go on a trip with his seminar group. Suzuki-san joins the discussion as they are talking about where to go. Tanaka-san suggests Nikko, but Suzuki-san insists on Hakone. Finally, Suzuki-san agrees to Nikko.

Flow-chart：

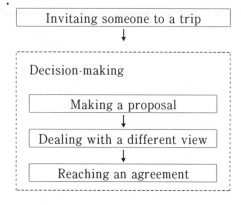

(1) In the seminar room

(2) In the seminar room (continued)

（1）―研究室で―

山　下：田中さん、冬休みどうするの。
田　中：ううん……、まだ決めてないんだけど。
　　　　どうして。
山　下：実は、毎年研究室の仲間で旅行するんだけどさ。
田　中：ふうん。
山　下：鈴木さんが今年はリサさんも誘えって、うるさいんだよ。
田　中：何よ。それじゃ、私はおまけってわけ。
山　下：いや、別にその、そういうわけじゃないんだけどさ。
田　中：失礼しちゃうわね、まったく。
山　下：まあ、そう怒らないでよ。
田　中：だって。
山　下：アニルさんも僕も田中さんたちが行ってくれるんなら楽しいさ。
田　中：そう。じゃ、ま、いいか。
　　　　リサさんも正月はこっちにいるはずよ。
山　下：そうか。
田　中：で、どこ行くの。
山　下：うん。それがね、……。

（２）―研究室で（つづき）―

鈴　木：よお、山下。
　　　　旅行のこと、決まったか。
山　下：あ、鈴木さん。
　　　　今、田中さんと相談してたんですけどね。
鈴　木：うん。
山　下：今のところ、箱根、金沢、日光って
　　　　ところが候補なんですけど。
鈴　木：ううん、金沢はちょっと遠いなあ。
　　　　2泊3日だろう。
山　下：そうですね。

　　　　＊　　　＊　　　＊

田　中：日光がいいんじゃないでしょうか。
　　　　1月なら、華厳の滝が凍ってて、きれいだそうですし。
鈴　木：だめだめ。せっかく旅行に行くのに、滝なんかつまらないよ。
　　　　箱根がいいな、箱根が。
田　中：箱根ですかあ。
鈴　木：やっぱりだれが何と言っても、正月は富士山に温泉に酒だよ。なあ、山下。
山　下：ええ、まあ、そうですね。
鈴　木：ロマンスカーなら、新宿から1時間ちょっとだし。
田　中：でも、日光だって、浅草から東武線の特急なら1時間半ちょっとですよ。
　　　　それに、日光ならスキーもできるし。
鈴　木：スキーなんて寒いだけだよ。
　　　　なあ、山下。
山　下：ええ、まあ。
田　中：(in a small voice) まったくもう、オジンなんだから。
鈴　木：えっ、何か言った。
田　中：いえ、別に。
田　中：ああ、そうそう。リサさん、日光行ったことないから、行きたいなんて、言っ
　　　　てたんですよね。
鈴　木：えっ、ほんと。
田　中：(as if talking to herself) それじゃ、私たちだけでも日光に行こうかな。
鈴　木：そうか。まあ、日光もいいかもしれないな。
　　　　うん、日光にしよう。

MC

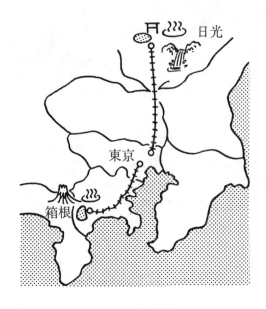

Report

＜リサさんへのメモ＞

リサさんへ

　きのう山下さんから、お正月に旅行するので、リサさんといっしょに来ないか、と誘われました。アニルさんや鈴木さんや木村研究室の人たちもいっしょだそうです。どこに行くかまだ決まっていないというので、日光がいいと提案しておきました。鈴木さんは、はじめ箱根のほうがいいと言っていたのに、リサさんが日光へ行きたいと言っていたと話したら、「日光もいいなあ」ですって！　２、３日中に山下さんが詳しい日程を知らせてくれると思うので、また連絡します。

　お正月は、日光でスキーをしましょう！　　　　　　　　田中より

New Words and Expressions

Words in the conversation

冬休み	ふゆやすみ	*winter holidays*
決める	きめる	*to decide*
毎年	まいとし	*every year*
仲間	なかま	*colleague, member*
旅行する	りょこうする	*to make a trip*
今年	ことし	*this year*
おまけ		*an extra, something thrown in*
怒る	おこる	*to get angry*
正月	しょうがつ	*New Year*
つづき		*continued*
決まる	きまる	*to be decided*
相談する	そうだんする	*to discuss, to consult*
今のところ	いまのところ	*for the time being*
箱根	はこね	place name
金沢	かなざわ	place name
日光	にっこう	place name
候補	こうほ	*proposed place, candidate*
遠い	とおい	*far*
２泊３日	にはくみっか	*staying three days and two nights*
華厳の滝	けごんのたき	*Kegon Fall*
凍る	こおる	*to freeze, to be frozen*
せっかく		*on purpose, especially*
滝	たき	*waterfall*
つまらない		*dull, boring*
やっぱり		*as one expected*
富士山	ふじさん	*Mt. Fuji*
温泉	おんせん	*hot spring*
ロマンスカー		*the Romance Car*（special express on Odakyu Line）
新宿	しんじゅく	place name in Tokyo
浅草	あさくさ	place name in Tokyo
東武線	とうぶせん	*Tobu Line*
特急	とっきゅう	*special express train*
スキー		*skiing*

MC

<Expressions in the conversation>

ふうん。 — *Hmm. / Oh? / Is that so?*

鈴木さんが今年はリサさんも誘えって、うるさいんだよ。
— *Suzuki insists on inviting Lisa this year.*

私はおまけってわけ。↗ — *Do you mean I am "a third wheel"?*

別にそういうわけじゃないんだけどさ。 — *It's not that I mean that, but...*

失礼しちゃうわね、まったく。 — *You really are rude.*

そう怒らないでよ。 — *Don't get so angry.*

じゃ、ま、いいか。 — *All right, then, I'll accept that.*

だめだめ。 — *No, no.*

せっかく旅行に行くのに、滝なんかつまらないよ。
— *We're going on a long-awaited trip — who wants to see a boring waterfall?*

だれが何と言っても、 — *no matter what anyone may say, in the final analysis*

まったくもう、オジンなんだから。 — *Gosh, what an old bore!*

オジン written in katakana is a special shortened form of **おじさん** (*uncle, strange man*) with the meaning of *old-fashioned, conservative man.*

いえ、別に。 — *Nothing special.*

Words in the report

メモ		memo
提案する	ていあんする	to propose, to suggest
はじめは		at the beginning
２、３日中に	に、さんにちちゅうに	in two or three days' time
詳しい	くわしい	detailed, full
日程	にってい	schedule ＝スケジュール
知らせる	しらせる	to inform
連絡する	れんらくする	to contact

210

Grammar Notes

I. ⑳ 〜（の）なら〈2〉: *if it is the case 〜/if 〜*

Examples

① A：車を買おうと思っています。
    I'm going to buy a car.

    B：そうですか。車を買う（の）なら、あの店が一番いいですよ。
    If you are going to buy a car, that shop is the best.

② A：その本、おもしろそうですね。
    That book looks interesting.

    B：ええ、お読みになる（の）なら、お貸ししますよ。
    If you are going to read it, I will lend it to you.

③ A：田中さんも行くそうですよ。
    I heard that Tanaka-san will go, too.

    B：そうですか。田中さんが行く（の）なら、私も行きたいです。
    Really? If Tanaka-san goes, I want to go, too.

【*Explanation*】

1. Use of 〜（の）なら

In lesson 4 we saw that [N]＋なら *if* indicates that something is taken up for further comment:

    A：せんたく機はどこですか。
    Where's the washing machine?

    B：ああ、せんたく機なら4階ですよ。
    The washing machine? It's on the 4th floor.

In the full structure {S₁}＋（の）なら{S₂}, {S₁}＋（の）なら again expresses an assumption *if* {S₁} *is the case*; {S₂} expresses a statement, request or offer etc. which depends on {S₁}＋（の）なら being true.

  〜（の）なら is normally used when taking up something for further comment, offering an opinion or advice etc. in the sense of *if what you say is true / if that is the case...*

For instance, in ①, B, having been told that A wants to buy a car, makes a comment advising A where best to go, and in ②, B offers to lend his book to A, who has expressed interest in it.

なら is attached to the forms of verbs, adjectives and [N]＋**だ** shown below; it is often used in the form of **の**（in casual speech **ん**）**なら**, which is a slightly more emphatic variant of 〜**なら**.

[V]	行く、行った、行かない 行かなかった、行っている 行っていない、……	（の）なら、〜
[A]	むずかしい むずかしくない むずかしかった むずかしくなかった	
[NA]	元気* げんき	なら、〜
	元気じゃない 元気だった 元気じゃなかった	（の）なら〜
[N]	学生* がくせい	なら、〜
	学生じゃない 学生だった 学生じゃなかった	（の）なら〜

* Note that **なら** is attached to the plain form, except for [N] **だ** and [NA] **だ**, in which case **だ** in dropped and **なら** attached directly.

2. Comparing 〜たら and 〜なら

Whereas in a **たら** sentence, {S₂} has to follow {S₁} in terms of time, this is not so in a **なら** sentence, as illustrated in the following example:

	{S₁}	{S₂}
✕	北海道に行ったら、	いっしょに行きましょう。
○	北海道に行くのなら、	いっしょに行きましょう。
	When you go to Hokkaido,	*let's go together.*

北海道に行く is a condition for いっしょに行きましょう, but there is no time sequence between the two sentences because the action of 北海道に行く and いっしょに行く will take place at the same time. Therefore たら cannot be used, but なら can. Now look at the following pair:

a. **オーストラリアに行ったら、車の免許をとったほうがいい。**

When you go to Australia, you'd better get a driving licence.

b. **オーストラリアに行くのなら、車の免許をとったほうがいい。**

If you're going to Australia, you'd better get a driving licence.

In both examples, the speaker assumes that the listener will go to Australia to live/work there; whereas the implication in the たら sentence is that the listener would get the licence IN Australia (sequence of time: after getting there), in the なら sentence the implication is that he would get it BEFORE getting there!

II. ～ても: *even if ～*

GN

Examples

① A：雨が降ったらどうしますか。　　*If it rains, what shall we do?*

B：雨が降っても行きますよ。　　*Even if it rains, we'll go.*

② いまはわからなくても、だんだんわかるようになりますよ。

Even if you don't understand (it) now, you will come to understand (it) gradually.

③ いくら覚えても、すぐ忘れてしまいます。

No matter how much I learn (it), I forget (it) right away.

④ リサさんは日曜日でも勉強する。

Lisa-san studies even on Sunday.

【*Explanation*】

〜ても（でも）is formed by adding も to the -te form of verbs, adjectives and ［N］＋だ. When attached to verbs and adjectives, it means *even if*, and when attached to a noun, *even*.

［V］	行って 行かなくて	
［A］	むずかしくて むずかしくなくて	も、〜
［NA］	便利で 便利じゃなくて	
［N］	学生で 学生じゃなくて	

After question words like いくら, どんなに, 何度, 何回, 何年, 〜ても means *no matter* 〈question word〉.

1. いくらさがしても、見つからない。
   No matter how much I look for it, I cannot find it.

2. この本は何度（何回）読んでもおもしろい。
   No matter how many times I read this book, it is interesting.

3. 何年住んでいても、新しい発見があります。
   No matter how many years I live here, I (still) find new things.

Ⅲ. 🔤　〜のに: *despite 〜／although 〜*

Examples

① がんばったのに、テストが悪かった。
Despite my hard work, my test (score) was poor.

② こんなに愛しているのに、どうして行ってしまうのですか。
Why are you going away, even though I love you so much?

③ アニルさんは寒いのに、半袖シャツを着ている。
In spite of the cold, Anil-san is wearing a short-sleeve shirt.

【*Explanation*】

1. Use of 〜のに

The meaning of **〜のに** *despite, although* is the exact opposite of that of **〜ので** *since, as* in that it indicates a strong contrast between the two halves of the sentence joined by **のに**. See how ① and ③ change when **〜ので** is used. ⇨L9GNⅢ

①' がんばったので、テストがよかった。
Since I studied hard, my test (score) was good.

②' 寒いので、アニルさんはセーターを着ている。
As it's cold, Anil-san is wearing a sweater.

〜のに is attached to the same form as **〜ので**:

[V]	見る、見た、見ない 見なかった、見ている 見ていない、……	
[A]	むずかしい むずかしくない むずかしかった むずかしくなかった	のに、～
[NA]	元気な* 元気じゃない 元気だった 元気じゃなかった	
[N]	学生な* 学生じゃない 学生だった 学生じゃなかった	

* **な**, NOT **だ**, is attached to the non-past positive of [NA] and [N].

2. Comparing ～ても and ～のに

Whereas ～のに contrasts statements of fact, ～ても basically contrasts hypothetical situations; in ～のに sentences {S₂} cannot express a supposition, intention, request or obligation, etc., but in ～ても sentences, it can:

a. **いっしょうけんめい勉強しても、大学院には入れないでしょう。**

Even if he studies hard, he won't be able to enter graduate school.

b. **いっしょうけんめい勉強したのに、大学院には入れなかった。**

Although he studied hard, he was unable to enter graduate school.

Compare also the pair below:

○ **難しくても、辞書を見ないでください。**

Don't look it up in a dictionary, even if it is difficult.

✕ **難しいのに、辞書を見ないでください。**

Ⅳ. 〜はずだ: *supposed to 〜／should 〜／ought to 〜*

Examples

① A：山田さんはまだ来ていませんね。
    Yamada-san hasn't come yet, has he?

  B：ええ、でも午後から会議がありますから、もうすぐ来るはずです。
    No, but since there's a meeting in the afternoon, he should be here soon.

② A：リサさんはアメリカに帰ったんですか。
    Did Lisa-san go back to America?

  B：ええ、夕べ。いまごろはもうアメリカに着いているはずですよ。
    Yes, last night. She should have arrived in America by now.

③ A：今度のゼミの発表は？
    Who is doing the next seminar?

  B：鈴木さんのはずです。彼、その準備で忙しそうでしたから。
    Suzuki-san, I suppose. He seemed to be busy with his preparations.

  A：リサさんじゃないんですか。
    Isn't it Lisa-san's turn?

  B：いいえ、リサさんじゃないはずです。先週発表したばかりです。
    No, it shouldn't be her turn. She only just gave a presentation last week.

④ A：バスはもうすぐ来ますか。
    Is the bus coming soon?

  B：ええ、5時半に来るはずです。
    Yes, it is due at 5:30.

GN

来るはずだ。

217

【*Explanation*】

1. The meaning indicated by はず

はず used in ①～④ expresses the speaker's judgment about the likelihood of an action or situation happening, on the basis of some objective information or knowledge. He is not simply making a guess, as with the more subjective **だろう**, but indicates that if his interpretation of his information or knowledge is correct, some situation or event ought to happen.

Let's look at some examples of the type of information or knowledge which the speaker uses for his judgment:

～はずだ		
information/knowledge	→	statement （unconfirmed probable occurrence）
午後から会議がある。	→	山田さんは来るはずだ。
夕べアメリカへ帰った。	→	アメリカに着いているはずだ。
鈴木さんは準備で忙しそうだった。	→	鈴木さんのはずだ。
リサさんは先週発表した。	→	リサさんではないはずだ。
時刻表（timetable）	→	5時半に来るはずだ。

The speakers interpretation of his information or knowledge relies on various factors; for instance, in ① speaker B knows that Yamada-san normally attends the meeting mentioned and can therefore be expected to come by the time the meeting begins, and ②, B has some idea of how long it takes to travel to the U.S.（by air）. Sometimes cultural knowledge is necessary for a correct interpretation, as in ④, where a statement with **はずだ** is only possible if one knows that in Japan, buses run according to schedule!

2. The structure using はずだ

はずだ is attached to the following forms:

	Plain form + はずだ	
	Plain form	
[V]	食べる、食べた、食べない 食べ<ruby>た</ruby>なかった、食べている 食べていない、……	
[A]	寒い 寒<ruby>さむ</ruby>かった 寒くない 寒くなかった	はずだ
[NA]	便利な 便利<ruby>べんり</ruby>だった 便利じゃない 便利じゃなかった	
[N]	試験の* 試験<ruby>しけん</ruby>だった 試験じゃない 試験じゃなかった	

*exception

　[NA] なはずだ
　　　便利なはずだ

　[N] のはずだ
　　　試験のはずだ

GN

V. ～わけだ: *That's why ～ ／ No wonder ～*

Examples

① A：山田<ruby>やまだ</ruby>さんが来<ruby>き</ruby>ていますね。　　　*Yamada-san's here, isn't he?*

　B：ええ、もうすぐ会議<ruby>かいぎ</ruby>があるんです。
　　　Yes, he is going to attend the meeting.

　A：ああ、それでいるわけですね。　　　*Oh, so that's why he's here.*

② A：今度のゼミの発表は鈴木さんよ。
The next seminar will be presented by Suzuki-san.

B：ああ、だから彼は忙しいわけだ。
Aha, that's why he is busy.

③ A：サニさんは日本に何年ぐらい住んでいるの。
How many years has Sani-san been in Japan?

B：10年ぐらい。
About 10 years.

A：日本語が上手なわけだ。
No wonder his Japanese is good.

いるわけだ。

【*Explanation*】

＜occurrence＋わけだ＞ is used when the speaker realizes that there is a good reason that explains some fact or occurrence.

～はずだ is used in statements when the speaker's judgements or guesses are based on confirmed information or knowledge. In contrast, ～わけだ is used when the speaker realizes that one fact or occurrence is the result of some other fact or occurrence. Look at ①～③.

～わけだ	
information/knowledge（reason） →	**statement**（confirmed occurrence）
もうすぐ会議がある。 →	山田さんがいるわけだ。
ゼミの発表は鈴木さんだ。 →	彼は忙しいわけだ。
日本に10年ぐらい住んでいる。 →	日本語が上手なわけだ。

〜わけだ is attached to the same forms as 〜はずだ, except for nouns, where [N] なわけだ／[N] というわけだ or [N] ってわけだ, but NOT [N] のわけだ is used.

Ⅵ. 実は、やっぱり、せっかく : sentence adverbs

Sentence adverbs are adverbs which describe the speaker's subjective attitude towards a whole sentence. Let's review other types of adverbs to see how they differ from sentence adverbs:

1. Adverbs of manner

1. 田中さんはゆっくり歩く。
   Tanaka-san walks slowly.

In this sentence, the adverb ゆっくり modifies 歩く to describe how (in what manner) Tanaka-san walks. Below are some more examples of this type of adverb.

2. まっすぐ行くと、バス停がありますよ。
   If you go straight on, you'll find a bus stop.

3. 早く起きられるように、早く寝よう。
   I'll go to bed early so that I'll be able to get up early.

2. Adverbs of degree or frequency

1. 授業のあと、ときどきサッカーをする。
   They sometimes play soccer after class.

2. 金沢はちょっと遠いなあ。
   Kanazawa is a bit too far away.

3. A：きのう、映画に行ったの。
   Did you go to the movies yesterday?

   B：うん、すごくおもしろかったよ。
   Yes, it was very interesting.

Modifying a verb or adjective, these adverbs indicate the degree or frequency of the action or state of the verb or adjective: ときどき indicates the frequency of playing soccer, ちょっと the degree of distance, and すごく the degree of being interesting.

221

3. Sentence adverbs

1. A：いま、よろしいでしょうか。

   May I talk to you now?

   B：どうしたの。

   What's the matter?

   A：実はご相談したいことがあるんです。

   Actually, I have something I'd like to talk over with you.

2. A：鈴木さんはいつも遅刻するんだよね。きっときょうも遅いよ。

   Suzuki-san always comes late. No doubt he'll be late today, too.

   B：まだ来ませんね。遅いな。

   He hasn't come yet. He's taking his time!

   A：あっ、来た来た。やっぱり鈴木さんは遅刻したよ。

   Here he comes. He's late, just as we expected.

3. A：せっかく旅行に行ったのに、かぜをひいてしまいました。

   I went to all the trouble to go on a trip, only to catch a cold.

   B：確か、田中さんもいっしょだったでしょう。

   If I remember rightly, Tanaka-san was with you.

   A：ええ、田中さんが薬をくれたんです。

   Yes, Tanaka-san gave me some medicine.

In this way, sentence adverbs (straight line) do not modify a verb or adjective indicating its manner, degree or frequency, but describe how the speaker feels or thinks about the facts or matters stated in the whole sentence (wavy line).

Conversation Notes

<General Information>

1. Useful information for planning a trip

When planning a trip, one needs to consider the destination (行き先), length (日程) and cost (予算). In Japanese, the length of stay is referred to as follows:

2泊3日	2 nights and 3 days
3泊4日	3 nights and 4 days
4泊5日	4 nights and 5 days

A guidebook is useful in helping to decide where to stay and what to see, but package tours are also available at travel agencies.

Reservations for train and bus tickets can be made at train or bus stations or at travel agencies. For special express trains (特急) and express trains (急行), there is a choice of various tickets that need to be bought in addition to the basic ticket (乗車券):

	寝台 sleeper		指定席 reserved seat		自由席 non-reserved seat	
	A寝台	B寝台	グリーン車 Green	普通車 Regular	グリーン車	普通車
特急列車 Special Express	特急券 A寝台券	特急券 B寝台券	特急券 指定席グリーン券	特急券	—	自由席特急券
急行列車 Express	急行券 A寝台券	急行券 B寝台券	急行券 指定席グリーン券	急行券 指定席券	急行券 自由席グリーン券	急行券

*特急券 *special express ticket* / 急行券 *express ticket*
片道乗車券 *one-way ticket* / 往復乗車券 *round-trip ticket*
グリーン車 *first-class carriage*

Excursion tickets (周遊券), which allow you to ride any train within a specified area (with some limitations) are often available for a flat fee. Information on such

tickets can be found in rail timetables/schedules (時刻表) which can be purchased at
bookshops or can be looked in train stations.

Discount rail tickets are available for students but these must be applied for in
advance at the school/university office.

2. Japanese inns

Japanese inns called **Ryokan** (旅館) are a type of traditional Japanese hotel.
Below is some useful information on things you ought to know when staying at a
Ryokan:

Rooms are usually Japanese-style (**tatami**) rooms, which sometimes do not have an
en-suite toilet or bath. Toilets are available on the same floor.

Like most Western-style hotels, a Ryokan will provide a freshly pressed **Yukata**
(a kimono-style garment for indoors use during your stay) as well as a towel,
toothbrush and shaver.

Breakfast and dinner are included in the price. These meals are usually served in
your room, although at some cheaper Ryokan you may be required to go to the dining
room. The refrigerator in your room is well stocked with alcoholic and soft drinks, for
which you are charged when you pay your bill, but warm sake etc. can also be ordered
with your meal.

After dinner, **Futons** will be laid down by Ryokan staff, who will put them away
again in the morning after you get up.

Ryokans tend to have at least two large Japanese baths, one for men and one for
women (風呂／浴場); in hot spring resorts, they also tend to have one or several
Rotenburo (露天風呂), large outdoor hot spring baths. (About how to take a bath, ⇨
L19CN4.)

The bill, which includes service and tax, is paid at the reception when leaving.

There is also a cheaper form of accommodation called 民宿 which are small
private pensions. Information on these is again available at travel agents and local
information offices.

<Strategies>

S-1. How to make a proposal
---

a. There are two ways to make a proposal. The first one can be called the direct way of proposing something (⇨L20CN S-4); in this case, you usually add a reason why you are proposing a place or course of action:

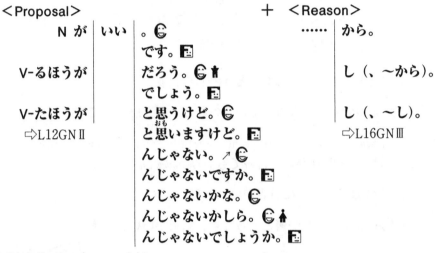

```
<Proposal>                        ＋  <Reason>
      N が ｜いい｜ 。G              ……  ｜から。
                  です。E
      V-るほうが    だろう。G ♂          し（、～から）。
                  でしょう。E
      V-たほうが    と思うけど。G          し（、～し）。
        ⇨L12GN Ⅱ   と思いますけど。E        ⇨L16GN Ⅲ
                  んじゃない。↗ G
                  んじゃないですか。E
                  んじゃないかな。G
                  んじゃないかしら。G ♀
                  んじゃないでしょうか。E
```

I think that ～ is a good idea,　　　　　　because...

① E 日光がいいんじゃないでしょうか。華厳の滝がきれいだそうですから。

② G 箱根がいいよ。富士山が見えるし、温泉もあるし。

③ G 新宿から行ったほうがいいんじゃない。↗　ロマンスカーなら、1時間ちょっとだし。

④ E リーさんも誘ったほうがいいと思いますけど。まだ日光へ行ったことがないそうですから。

CN

b. The second way of making a proposal is less direct in that you ask the other party's opinion:

＜Proposal＞

N は	どう	。↗ 
N なんて		ですか。
		かな。
V（っていう）のは		かしら。
		でしょうか。
V-たら		かと思うけど。
		かと思うんですけど。

What do you think about 〜 ? ／ How about 〜 ?

① 日光でスキーなんて、どうかしら。

② 箱根で温泉に入るっていうのはどうかと思うんですけど。

When you want to make your point forcefully, you can use expressions such as **ぜったいに** *(absolutely),* **だれが何と言っても** *(Whatever anyone might say):*

③ 私はぜったいに日光がいいと思います。

④ やっぱりだれが何と言っても、箱根がいいよ。

S-2. How to voice disagreement

a. When you disagree with what a junior has said, you can indicate your disagreement directly as in the underlined part below. You can also add a reason why you disagree, or give an alternative view. See the following examples:

①　田中：日光がいいんじゃないでしょうか。華厳の滝がきれいだそうですし。

　　鈴木：だめだめ。滝なんかつまらないよ。箱根がいいな。

②　山下：時間がかかるので、タクシーを使ったらどうかと思うんですけど。

　　鈴木：いや、時間がかかっても、タクシーよりケーブルカーに乗ったほうがいいよ。安いし、景色 *(scenery)* もいいし。

In the case of a decision-making meeting, the word 反対（はんたい）*(I'm) against (it)* can be used:

③　A：飛行機で行ったほうがいいと思います。

　　B：反対です。フェリーのほうが安いし、楽しいですよ。
　　　　I have an objection.

Chairman：では、採決をとります。反対の人は、手をあげてください。
　　　　　　Let's take a vote, then.

b. However, you must be careful when you want to show disagreement with a senior. Direct negative comments like だめ, よくない, つまらない, 反対だ should be avoided. The Japanese usually voice their disagreement diplomatically by first voicing acceptance to what the senior has said with そうですね once; only then they will indicate their objection with *but*（でも, しかし, 〜けど, 〜が, etc.), followed by their differing opinion:

①　鈴木⬇：箱根がいいよ。温泉があるし。

　　山下⬆：そうですね。確かに温泉もいいですけど、スキーのほうが
　　　　　　みんなで楽しめるんじゃないでしょうか。

②　先輩⬇：次のミーティングは水曜日がいいな。

　　後輩⬆：そうですね。でも、できればウィークデーじゃないほうが
　　　　　　いいと思うんですけど。たとえば、土曜とか。

c. In casual speech, you can show disagreement by intonation or facial expression; however, this is rather rude:

①Ⓒ鈴木：箱根がいいな、箱根が。

　　田中：箱根ですかあ。↗

②ⒸA：バスで行ったらどうかと思うんだけど。
　　B：ええっ↗、バス。↗

CN

227

S-3. How to support someone's view

When you agree with what someone else has said, you can indicate your support with the following expressions:

そうですね。🖪｜〈view〉｜です（よ）ね。🖪
｜｜だ（よ）ね。😀🕴
そうだね。😀🕴｜｜（よ）ね。😀👤
｜（それは）いい考えだと｜思います🖪
そうね。😀｜（私も）そう｜思うよ。😀🕴
｜｜思うわ。😀👤
｜（私も）賛成｜です。🖪
｜｜。😀

① 鈴木▣：金沢はちょっと遠いなあ。

　　山下▣：そうですね。遠いですよね。

② 先輩▣：バスで行ったらどうかと思うんだけど。

　　後輩▣：そうですね。私もそう思います。

③🖪A：この場合、最後までやったほうがいいでしょう。

　　B：その通りだと思います。
　　　You are quite right. / Exactly!

④😀A：水曜より金曜のほうがいいよ。次の日が休みだから。🕴

　　B：そうね。賛成。👤
　　　Yes. I agree.

⑤😀A：箱根より日光のほうがいいんじゃないかしら。👤

　　B：そうだね。僕もそう思うよ。🕴

228

S-4. How to ask for someone's approval

When you want to get someone else to approve or support what you say, you can use the following expressions:

①📧A：やっぱり東京のほうがいいと思うんですけど、<u>いかがですか</u>。

　　B：そうですね。

②📧A：XよりYのほうがいいでしょう。<u>そう思いませんか</u>。

　　B：ええ、そうですね。

③👥田中：タクシーを呼んだほうがいいわよ。<u>ね</u>。↗ 👤

　　山下：うん。そうだね。👤

④👥鈴木⬇：正月は富士山に温泉に酒だよ。<u>なあ</u>↘、<u>山下</u>。👤

　　山下🔼：ええ、まあ、そうですね。

そう思いませんか／そうでしょう↗ *Don't you think so?* is stronger than **いかがですか／どうですか** *How do you think?*

S-5. How to avoid a definite statement

CN

When you are unable to support a senior's opinion but do not want to explicitly say so, the following ambiguous statements are useful:

①📧A：やっぱり車なら、○○○ですよね。

　　B：<u>はあ</u>。↘ <u>そうですね</u>。↘

②📧A：Bさんはどう思います。↗

　　B：ええと……、そうですね。↘ <u>ちょっと簡単には言えないんじゃないかと思いますが</u>。

③👥鈴木⬇：スキーなんて寒いだけだよ。なあ、山下。👤

　　山下🔼：<u>ええ、まあ</u>。

④ⓒ田中：山下さんはどう思ってるのよ。♟

山下：ううん↘、……。むずかしいなあ。

まとめ 6

A. GRAMMAR

Ⅰ. Verb forms
Ⅱ. Similar sentences with the different meaning
Ⅲ. Adverbs
Ⅳ. は and が in complex sentences

B. CONVERSATION

Ⅰ. Summary of Conversational Strategies

Ⅱ. Additional Information
1. Use of 〜んじゃない
2. Male and female speech（2）

A. Grammar

I. Verb forms

Below is a chart of the verb forms we have come across for each group of verbs:

Group I	Plain form			Polite form
		-nai f.	-ta f.	-masu f.
Ordinary v.	飲む _の	飲まない	飲んだ	飲みます
Potential v.	飲める	飲めない	飲めた	飲めます
Imperative f.	飲め	飲むな	—	飲みなさい
-(y)oo f.	飲もう	—	—	飲みましょう
Passive v.	飲まれる	飲まれない	飲まれた	飲まれます
Causative v.	飲ませる	飲ませない	飲ませた	飲ませます
Honorific v. Passive honorific f.	めしあがる 飲まれる	めしあがらない 飲まれない	めしあがった 飲まれた	めしあがります 飲まれます
Humble v.	いただく	いただかない	いただいた	いただきます

Group II	Plain form			Polite form
		-nai f.	-ta f.	-masu f.
Ordinary v.	見る _み	見ない	見た	見ます
Potential v.	見られる	見られない	見られた	見られます

Imperative f.	見ろ	見るな	–	見なさい
-(y)oo f.	見よう	–	–	見ましょう
Passive v.	見られる	見られない	見られた	見られます
Causative v.	見させる	見させない	見させた	見させます
Honorific v.	ごらんになる	ごらんにならない	ごらんになった	ごらんになります
Honorific v. Passive honorific f.	ごらんになる 見られる	ごらんにならない 見られない	ごらんになった 見られた	ごらんになります 見られます
Humble v.	はいけんする	はいけんしない	はいけんした	はいけんします

Group Ⅲ	Plain form			Polite form
		-nai f.	-ta f.	-masu f.
Ordinary v.	する	しない	した	します
Potential v.	できる	できない	できた	できます
Imperative f.	しろ	するな	–	しなさい
-(y)oo f.	しよう	–	–	しましょう
Passive v.	される	されない	された	されます
Causative v.	させる	させない	させた	させます
Honorific v. Passive honorific f.	なさる される	なさらない されない	なさった された	なさいます されます
Humble v.	いたす	いたさない	いたした	いたします

まとめ

	Plain form			Polite form
	-nai f.	-ta f.		-masu f.
Ordinary v.	来る	来ない	来た	来ます
Potential v.	来られる	来られない	来られた	来られます
Imperative f.	来い	来るな	—	来なさい
-(y)oo f.	来よう	—	—	来ましょう
Passive v.	来られる	来られない	来られた	来られます
Causative v.	来させる	来させない	来させた	来させます
Honorific v. Passive honorific f.	いらっしゃる 来られる	いらっしゃらない 来られない	いらっしゃった 来られた	いらっしゃいます 来られます
Humble v.	まいる	まいらない	まいった	まいります

Ⅱ. Similar sentences with the different meaning

Work out how the sentences in each group differ from one another. Pay attention to the use of particles and to who is doing things to whom.

1. a. アニルさんは木村先生に食事にさそわれました。

   b. 木村先生はアニルさんを食事にさそわれました。

2. a. 林さんに紹介されました。

   b. 林さんが紹介されました。

3. a. 木村先生にそう言われました。

   b. 木村先生がそう言われました。

4. a. アニルさんはあした来られますか。

   b. 勉強しているとき、いつもアニルさんに来られます。

5. a. 名前は日本語で書きますか。

   b. 名前は日本語で書けますか。

   c. 名前は日本語で書かれますか。

6. a. 父が食べろと言った。

   b. 父が食べようと言った。

7. a. 来週帰ろうと思います。

   b. 来週帰ると思います。

8. a. アニルさんが行かせたんです。

   b. アニルさんを行かせたんです。

9. a. ちょっと待て。

   b. ちょっと待って。

   c. ちょっと待ってて。

10. a. これ、やってほしいんだけど。

    b. これ、やりたいんだけど。

    c. これ、やってもらいたいんだけど。

Here are the correct answers together with the translations of the sentences in II:

1. a. *Anil-san was invited to dinner by Kimura-sensee.* (Passive)
   b. *Kimura-sensee invited Anil-san to dinner.* (Honorific)

2. a. *I was introduced to Hayashi-san (by someone).* (Passive)
   or *I was introduced (to someone) by Hayashi-san.* (Passive)
   b. *Hayashi-san was introduced (by someone).* (Passive)
   or *Hayashi-san introduced (someone).* (Honorific)

3. a. *I was told so by Kimura-sensee.* (Passive)
   b. *Kimura-sensee said so.* (Honorific)

4. a. *Will you come tomorrow, Anil-san?* (Honorific)
   or *Can you come tomorrow?* (Potential)
   b. *Anil-san always comes when I am studying (and it bothers me).*
   (Passive)

まとめ

5. **a.** *Do you write your name in Japanese?*
   b. *Can you write your name in Japanese?*（Potential）
   c. *Do you write your name in Japanese?*（Honorific）

6. **a.** *Father said, 'Eat.'*（Imperative）
   b. *Father said, 'Let's eat.'*（-(y)oo f.）

7. **a.** *I would like to go back next week.*（-(y)oo f.）
   b. *I think s/he will go back next week.*

8. **a.** *Anil-san made me/someone go.*（Causative）
   b. *I made Anil-san go.*（Causative）

9. **a.** *Wait a moment.*（Imperative）
   b. *Wait a moment please.*（Polite request）
   c. *Wait a moment please.*（Polite request）

   待ってて is a shortened form of 待っていて（ください）.

10. **a.** *I want you to do this.*
    b. *I want to do this.*
    c. *I want you to do this.*

Ⅲ. Adverbs

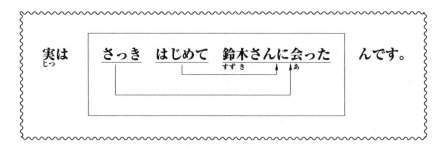

The above illustration shows that the sentence is composed of an outer frame（the part enclosed by the wavy line）and an inner core（the part enclosed by the straight line）. The outer frame holds the whole sentence together and describes the speaker's attitude or feeling about the objective fact which is found in the inner core.

Adverbs can thus be divided into two groups: one that modifies an objective fact（the core of the sentence）, and another that expresses the speaker's attitude or feeling（the outer frame）.

さっき *a little while ago* and はじめて *for the first time* modify an objective fact (鈴木さんに会った) by explaining when and how the meeting took place.

By contrast, 実は *in fact* expresses the speaker's attitude about the matter under discussion.

1. Sentential adverbs

The following are examples of adverbs that show the speaker's attitude.

1. 実はまだ準備ができていないんです。
   To tell the truth, I haven't finished the preparation yet.

2. ぜひ来てほしい。
   I strongly want you to come.

3. ええと、確か、５２の３１８１だと思います。
   Well, if I remember correctly, I think it's 52-3181.

2. Adverbs that modify the matter under discussion

1) ＜Adverbs of manner＞

1. いっしょに郵便局へ行きました。
   We went to the post office together.

2. 早く起きてください。　　　　　*Get up early.*

3. すぐ連絡します。　　　　　*I'll contact you straight away.*

4. 鈴木さんにはじめて会いました。
   I met Suzuki-san for the first time.

5. ここをまっすぐ行くとバス停があります。
   If you go straight on, you'll find the bus stop.

6. ゆっくり弱い火で何時間も煮る。
   Boil slowly for several hours on low heat.

7. レポートがなかなか書けない。
   I find it difficult to write the report.

8. 口を大きく開けて。　　　　　*Open your mouth wide.*

9. 本当に安かったよ。　　　　　*It was really cheap.*

まとめ

2 ）＜Adverbs of degree: *how much/ how far, etc.*＞

1. そでが<u>ちょっと</u>長い。 　　　*The sleeves are a bit long.*

2. <u>少々</u>お待ちください。 　　　*Please be so kind as to wait a little while.*

3. <u>ずいぶん</u>大きいですね。 　　　*It's quite big.*

4. <u>すごく</u>重かった。 　　　*It was very heavy.*

5. <u>非常に</u>おもしろい。 　　　*It's very interesting.*

6. <u>あまり</u>おもしろくありません。 　　*It isn't very interesting.*

7. <u>ぜんぜん</u>踊れません。 　　　*I can't dance at all.*

8. 木村先生は<u>とても</u>きびしい先生です。
　　Kimura-sensee is a very strict teacher.

9. <u>もっと</u>広い部屋に住みたい。 　　*I want to live in a bigger room.*

10. 駅は<u>かなり</u>遠いですよ。 　　　*The station is quite far.*

11. <u>そんなに</u>遠くないですよ。 　　　*It's not so far.*

12. お酒を<u>たくさん</u>飲んだでしょう。 　*You must have drunk a lot.*

13. 日本語の授業は<u>だいたい</u>わかります。
　　I mostly understand my Japanese class.

14. <u>できるだけ</u>日本語で話そうと思っている。
　　I intend to speak in Japanese as much as possible.

15. バスが<u>一番</u>便利です。
　　The bus is the most convenient (means of transport).

3 ）＜Adverbs of frequency: *how often*＞

1. <u>ときどき</u>映画を見に行きます。 　*I sometimes go to see a movie.*

2. A：<u>よく</u>東京に行きますか。 　　*Do you often go to Tokyo.*

　　B：<u>めったに</u>行きません。 　　　*I rarely go to Tokyo.*

238

4 ） ＜Adverbs of time: *when/how long/ in what order*＞

1. 先ほどお電話した山下ですが。
  (さき) (でんわ) (やました)
  This is Yamashita; I rang a little while ago.

2. 後でご連絡ください。　　　　*Please contact me later.*
  (あと) (れんらく)

3. 先に車にお乗りください。　　*Please go ahead and get in the car.*
  (さき) (くるま) (の)

4. はじめにひらがなを習って、次に漢字を習いました。
  (なら) (つぎ) (かんじ)
  First, we learned Hiragana, then we learned Kanji.

5. 近いうちに結婚する。
  (ちか) (けっこん)
  We'll get married in the near future.

6. あと少しで終わります。　　　*I'll finish it soon.*
  (すこ) (お)

7. ６年間ずっとこのアパートに住んでいる。
  (ろくねんかん) (す)
  I've been living in this apartment for 6 long years.

8. 毎朝ジョギングをしています。　　*I jog every morning.*
  (まいあさ)

IV. は and が in complex sentences

Read the following sentence, and tell who took off the shirt and who washed it.

アニルさんはリサさんがぬいだシャツを洗いました。
(あら)

The structure of this sentence is:

> アニルさんは　｜　リサさんが　ぬいだ　[シャツ]　｜　を　洗いました

　　[N] が usually modifies the verb which directly follows it, while [N] は modifies the final predicate.

　　リサさんが modifies ぬいだ, アニルさんは modifies 洗いました, and the sentence means *Anil-san washed the shirt which Lisa-san took off.*

If it is clear from the situation who washed the shirt, that person's name can be omitted:

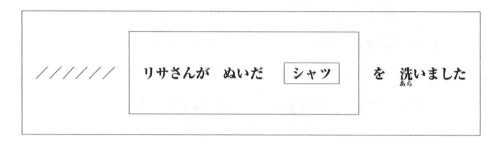

→ リサさんがぬいだシャツを洗いました。

(I/You/He/She) washed the shirt which Lisa-san took off.

On the other hand, the next sentence (structure) indicates that the person who is the topic (= Anil-san) took off the shirt and washed it.

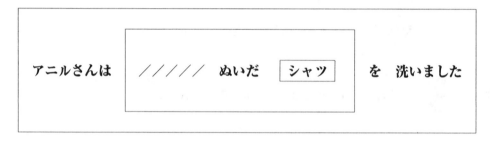

→ アニルさんはぬいだシャツを洗いました。

Anil-san washed the shirt which he took off.

1. Read (1) and (2), and tell who washed Lisa-san's shirt.

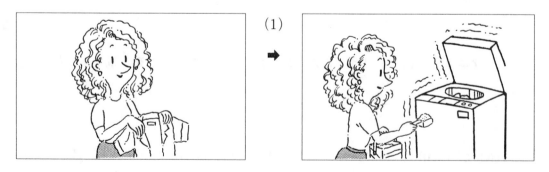

(1)

(1) リサさんはぬいだシャツを洗った。

Lisa-san washed the shirt which she had taken off.

（2）リサさんがぬいだシャツを洗った。

(Lisa-san's boy friend) washed the shirt which she (= Lisa-san) took off.

2. Tell who cried at the airport.

（1）私は飛行機に乗るとき泣いた。

（2）私が飛行機に乗るとき泣いた。

（1）私は飛行機に乗るとき泣いた。

When I was getting on the airplane, I cried.

（2）私が飛行機に乗るとき泣いた。

When I was getting on the airplane, (my girl friend) cried.

Ⅰ. *Summary of Conversational Strategies*

1. Factual information

☐ ☐ How to ask about the patient's
condition　　　⇨L22 S-3

：いかがですか／どうですか
どうなさったんですか
どんな具合いですか。

2. Judgement

☐ ☐ How to admit one's mistake
⇨L21 S-3

：そうだったんですか。
すみません。これから気をつけます。

☐ ☐ How to make a proposal
⇨L24 S-1

：Vたほうが ｜ いいんじゃないかな。
Vるほうが ｜ いいと思うけど。
Nなんて ｜ どうかな。
Vたら ｜ どうかと思うけど。

☐ ☐ How to voice disagreement
⇨L24 S-2

：だめだめ。〈N〉なんかつまらないよ。
〜ても、〜たほうがいいよ。
私は、反対です。
ええっ↗、Nですか。↗

☐ ☐ How to support someone's
view　　　⇨L24 S-3

：そうですね。／そうだね。

☐ ☐ How to ask for someone's
approval　　　⇨L24 S-4

：そうでしょう。↗
そう思いません。↗
なあ↘、山下。↗

☐ ☐ How to avoid a definite statement
⇨L24 S-5

：はあ。↘ そうですね。↘
ええ、まあ↘
ううん。むずかしいですね。

3. Emotions

☐ ☐ How to cheer up the patient
⇨L22 S-4

：心配しなくても、大丈夫ですよ。
すぐ元気になりますよ。
どうぞお大事に。

☐ ☐ How to complain　　⇨L21 S-1

：あのう　申しわけありませんが、テレ
ビの音が。
テレビの音をもう少し小さくしてくれ
ないかな。

☐ ☐ How to express anger　⇨L21 S-2

：頭に来るよ。
いいかげんにしろよ。

4. Actions

☐ ☐ How to admit a mistake   ：そうだったんですか。
         ⇨L21 S-3   すみません。これから気をつけます。

☐ ☐ How to apologize —2. ⇨L21 S-4 ：申しわけありません。📄
                     すみません。
                     ごめんなさい。🄲

☐ ☐ How to make a request   ：申しわけありませんが、
         ⇨L23 S-2   Vていただけませんか。📄⬆
                悪いけど、Vて │ もらえないかな。🄲
                わる   │ くれませんか。
                             │ いただきたいんです。

☐ ☐ How to persuade someone   ：そこを何とかお願いできませんか。
    to accept your request ⇨L23 S-5

5. Social formulas

☐ ☐ How to give a present ⇨L22 S-2 ：つまらないものですが。(L19 S-2)
                       あの、これ、どうぞ。
                     これ、お見舞いなんですけど。
                         み ま

☐ ☐ Asking someone to be more ：気をつけてくださいね。
    careful   ⇨L22 S-5   き
                       注意してくださいね。
                     ちゅう い

☐ ☐ How to refuse a request politely ：申しわけありませんが、
         ⇨L23 S-3   ちょっと……。📄⬆
                悪いけど、ちょっと……。
                わる
                お役に立てなくて、申しわけありませ
                やく た
                ん。

☐ ☐ How to withdraw a request   ：あ、そうですか。どもすみませんでした。
    that is refused   ⇨L23 S-4   いいえ、どうもおじゃましました。

6. Communication strategies

☐ ☐ How to start a conversation
    （9）Visiting a sick person   ：具合いは、どうですか。
                  ⇨L22 S-1   ぐ あ
    （10）Making a request   S-1a ：＜problem＞ んですけど。📄
                ⇨L23 S-1b   ＜time＞、お時間ございますか。📄⬆
                            [N] おわかりになりますか。📄⬆
                           じ かん

まとめ

II. *Additional Information*

1. Use of 〜んじゃない

1. Falling intonation
　〜んじゃない with falling intonation indicates that speaker's negative judgement, prohibition, etc.

１）[N]なんじゃない
　　　彼は、病気なんじゃない。↘　　　　　*I don't think that he is ill.*

２）[A] んじゃない
　　　① 悲しいんじゃない。↘　　　　　*I'm not sad.*

　　　② 彼が悪いんじゃない。↘　　　　*I think that it's not his fault.*

３）[NA] んじゃない
　　　きらいなんじゃない。↘ 好きなんだ。　*I don't hate it. I like it.*

４）[V]んじゃない
　　　① それ、食べるんじゃない。↘　　＝食べるな。
　　　　Don't eat it!

　　　② 走るんじゃない。↘　　　　　＝走るな。
　　　　Don't run!

2. Rising intonation

１）Opinion
　〜んじゃない↗ puts the speaker's opinion to the listener in question form. It means something rather like 〜と思う *(I think 〜)*. The polite form of 〜んじゃない is 〜んじゃありませんか. Recall the words of the passer-by in Lesson 12,「歩いて行くより、バスで行った方がいいんじゃないかしら。」.

　　　　高いんじゃ｜ない。↗　　　　　*Isn't it expensive?*
　　　　　　　　　｜ありませんか。↗

〜**ない** can occur twice in a sentence; 「**高くないんじゃない**。↗」 *it's not expensive, is it?*, **高くない** being the negative form of **高い**, and 〜**んじゃない** indicating the speaker's opinion.

> A：ね、この部屋ちょっと暑いんじゃない。↗
> *Hey, don't you think this room is a bit hot?*

> B：そうかしら。　　　　　　　　*I don't think so.*

2）Confirmation

When 〜**んじゃない** is attached to a statement of fact, it is used as a confirmation like a tag question in English.

> ① A：あした、漢字のテストがあるんじゃない。↗
> *Isn't there going to be Kanji test tomorrow, is it?*

> B：えっ。そうかしら。
> *What?! Really?*

> ② A：鈴木さん、きょうちょっと元気じゃないんじゃない。↗
> *Mr. Suzuki doesn't look well today, does he?*

> B：そうね。どうしたのかしら。
> *No. I wonder what's wrong.*

2. Male and female speech (2)

⇨まとめ5BⅡ

In casual speech, men and women tend to use some different expressions, especially in situations when they feel that they should sound typically *male* or *female*; Let's review some of these below. and look at some further differences:

1. Ending particles
1）Women tend to omit **だ** before **ね/よ**.

> ① いい天気だね。♂　　　　　　*Fine weather, isn't it?*
> 　 いい天気ね。♀

> ② この辞書、便利だよ。♂　　　　*This dictionary is useful.*
> 　 この辞書、便利よ。♀

2) Women tend to add **わ** to a statement.

 ① **あ、雨だ。**   *It's raining.*
  あら、雨だわ。 ♀

 ② **これ、おいしいね。**   *This is delicious, isn't it?*
  これ、おいしいわね。 ♀

 ③ **授業が始まるよ。**   *The class is going to start.*
  授業が始まるわよ。 ♀

3) Men tend to use **な** instead of **ね**.

 ① **そうだね。** ↗   *Yes, I agree.*
  そうだな。 ↗ ♂
  cf. **そうね。** ↗ ♀

 ② **悪いね。**   *Sorry.*
  悪いな。 ♂
  cf. **悪いわね。** ♀

4) Women tend to use **かしら** instead of **かな**.

 ① **あの人、学生かな。**   *I wonder if that person is a student.*
  あの人、学生かしら。 ♀

 ② **リサさん、来るかな。**   *I wonder if Lisa will come.*
  リサさん、来るかしら。 ♀

5) Men tend to add **か** or **かい** to a question.

 ① **あした、休み。** ↗   *Is tomorrow a holiday?*
  あした、休みか。 ♂

 ② **電話番号、わかる。** ↗   *Do you know the telephone number?*
  電話番号、わかるかい。 ♂

2. Sentence endings

1) Men tend to use the imperative form instead of [V(base)] **なさい** or [V-nai] **で**.

 ① **早く寝なさい。**   *Hurry up and go to sleep.*
  早く寝ろ。 ♂

② かぎ、忘れないでよ。　　　　　*Don't forget the key.*
　 かぎ、忘れるなよ。🚹

2）Men sometimes make a request with [V-te] くれ.

　　① ちょっと手伝って。　　　　　　*Can you give me a hand?*
　　　 ちょっと手伝ってくれ。🚹

　　② だれにも言わないでよ。　　　　 *Don't tell anyone.*
　　　 だれにも言わないでくれよ。🚹

3）Women tend to use 〜の insted of 〜んだ.

　　①-1　A：どうしたんだ。🚹　　　　 *What's the matter?*
　　　　　B：頭が痛いんだ。🚹　　　　 *I have a headache.*

　　②-2　A：どうしたの。
　　　　　B：頭が痛いの。🚺

4）Women tend to use 〜でしょう insted of 〜だろう.

　　①-1　A：リサさんは。　　　　　　 *Where's Lisa?*
　　　　　B：たぶん教室だろう。🚹　　 *In the classroom, I think.*

　　①-2　A：リサさんは。
　　　　　B：たぶん教室でしょう。🚺

　　②-1　A：パーティに行くだろう。↗ 🚹 *You're going to the party, aren't*
　　　　　B：うん。　　　　　　　　　　　 *you.*

　　②-2　A：パーティに行くでしょう。↗ 🚺
　　　　　B：うん。

3. Words

Men tend to use some different words in casual speech:

私→おれ／ぼく 🚹
ごはん→めし 🚹
食べる→くう 🚹　　　 etc.

まとめ

Appendix

I. Grammar Check

文法（ぶんぽう）チェック L17

Read the Grammar Notes of Lesson 17, and check how well you have understood it. Choose the most appropriate statement.

1　a）　いいカメラをほしい。
　　b）　　　カメラが
　　c）　　　カメラで

2　a）　田中さんはカメラがほしいです。
　　b）　　　　　　　　　　ほしいます。
　　c）　　　　　　　　　　ほしいと言っています。

3　a）　写真をとることがほしいんですが。
　　b）　　　　とってほしいんですが。
　　c）　　　　とりたいんですが。

4　　　A：何を読んでいるんですか。
　　　　B：タイ語の本です。
　　a）　A：ちょっと見せてください。難し　　そうですね。
　　b）　　　　　　　　　　　　　　難しい
　　c）　　　　　　　　　　　　　　難しいだ

5　a）　ここへ来いと言いわれました。
　　b）　　　　　　　言られました。
　　c）　　　　　　　言われました。

6　a）　リサさんは田中さんに英語の質問をされました。
　　b）　　　　　田中さんが
　　c）　　　　　田中さんを

7　a）　どろぼうに私のお金をとりました。
　　b）　私はどろぼうにお金をとられました。
　　c）　私はどろぼうがお金をとりました。

8　　　Q：コーヒーと紅茶と、どちらにしますか。
　　a）　A：どちらが　いいです。
　　b）　　　どちらで
　　c）　　　どちらでも

文法（ぶんぽう）チェック **L18**

Read the Grammar Notes of Lesson 18, and check how well you have understood it. Choose <u>the most appropriate statement.</u>

1　a）　先生の仕事をお手伝いました。
　　b）　　　　　　お手伝いしました。
　　c）　　　　　　お手伝いにしました。

2　a）　私は図書館で本を借りました。
　　b）　　　　　　　　　お借りしました。
　　c）　　　　　　　　　お借りになりました。

3　　　　＜先生の家に電話をかける＞
　　a）　A：もしもし、リサとおっしゃいますが。　　　　B：はい。
　　b）　　　　　　　　　もうしますが。
　　a）　A：先生はいらっしゃいますか。
　　b）　　　　　おりますか。

4　a）　日本語で論文を書くことを　　できますか。
　　b）　　　　　　書くことが
　　c）　　　　　　書けることが

5　a）　音楽が好きですかどうですか聞きました。
　　b）　　　好きだかどうか
　　c）　　　好きかどうか

6　a）　先生がどこにいらっしゃるを　　　　知っていますか。
　　b）　　　　　　いらっしゃるか
　　c）　　　　　　いらっしゃるかどうか

7　a）　きのうはじめて歌舞伎を見ましたが、おもしろいですね。
　　b）　　　はじめに
　　c）　　　はじめは

8　a）　五人しかいない。
　　b）　五人だけいる。
　　c）　五人もいる。

9　a）　三人しかいない。
　　b）　三人だけいる。
　　c）　三人もいる。

文法（ぶんぽう）チェック L19

Read the Grammar Notes of Lesson 19, and check how well you have understood it.
Choose <u>the most appropriate statement.</u>

1　a）　あしたは東京へ行き　つもりです。
　　b）　　　　　　　行く
　　c）　　　　　　　行こう

2　a）　テレビを見るながらごはんを食べます。
　　b）　　　　見てながら
　　c）　　　　見ながら

3　　　A：休みは家族で旅行をしました。
　　a）　B：じゃあ、楽しかったです。
　　b）　　　　楽しかったんです。
　　c）　　　　楽しかったでしょう。

4　a）　A：ねえ、あしたは休みです。
　　b）　　　　　　　　　　休みでしょう。
　　　　　B：そうですよ。

5　a）　木村先生が書かれた　論文を読みましたか。
　　b）　　　　　　お書きした
　　c）　　　　　　書いた

6　a）　わあ、こんな　食べられません。
　　b）　　　　こんなに
　　c）　　　　そんな
　　d）　　　　そんなに
　　e）　　　　あんな
　　f）　　　　あんなに

7　a）　今週の土曜日にでも行きませんか。
　　b）　　　　土曜日でもに

8　a）　ニュースで聞いたんですが、きょうは円が安い　そうですね。
　　b）　　　　　　　　　　　　　　　　　　　　安いだ

9　a）　A：山田さんが帰りそうですよ。
　　b）　　　　　　帰る
　　　　　B：いつですか。
　　　　　A：あしたの朝だそうです。

文法（ぶんぽう）チェック L20

Read the Grammar Notes of Lesson 20, and check how well you have understood it.
Choose the most appropriate statement.

1　a）モンゴル料理を一度食べることがありました。
　　b）　　　　　　　　　　　食べることがあります。
　　c）　　　　　　　　　　　食べたことがあります。

2　a）去年インドへ行ったことがありますか。
　　b）　　　　　　行きましたか。
　　c）　　　　　　行きますか。

3　a）スイッチを入れるば、動きます。
　　b）　　　　　入れば、
　　c）　　　　　入れれば、

4　a）駅に着いたら、電話してください。
　　b）　　着けば、
　　c）　　着くと、

5　a）となりの部屋が静かだときは、よく勉強できます。
　　b）　　　　　　静かのときは、
　　c）　　　　　　静かなときは、

6　　　「いまうちにいますので、センターへ行くとき電話します。」
　　a）この人はうちで　　電話する。
　　b）　　　　　センターで
　　c）　　　　　センターかうちかどちらで電話するかわからない。

7　　　A：かぎはどこ。
　　a）B：かばんの中だかもしれない。
　　b）　　　　　中　かもしれない。
　　c）　　　　　中にかもしれない。

8　a）手紙の書き方が　わからない。
　　b）　　書く方が
　　c）　　書いてかたが

9　a）この料理はからすぎて、おいしい。
　　b）　　　　　　　　　　おいしくない。
　　c）　　　　　　　　　　ちょうどいい。

Read the Grammar Notes of Lesson 21, and check how well you have understood it. Choose <u>the most appropriate statement.</u>

1　a）　お金がなくて、買えません。
　　b）　　　　　　　買いません。
　　c）　　　　　　　友だちに借ります。

2　a）　頭が痛くて、　きょうは仕事を休みます。
　　b）　　　痛いので、
　　c）　　　痛いと、

3　a）　遅くなったので、すみません。
　　b）　遅くなったから、
　　c）　遅くなって、

4　a）　A：きのうのこの話ですが。
　　b）　　　　　　その話
　　c）　　　　　あの話
　　　　B：ああ、休みの旅行のことですね。
　　　　A：ええ。

5　a）　車を買ったので、便利　　　なりました。
　　b）　　　　　　　　便利に
　　c）　　　　　　　　便利ように

6　a）　毎日テレビを見ているので、日本語がわかるようになった。
　　b）　　　　　　　　　　　　　　　わかるようにできた。
　　c）　　　　　　　　　　　　　　　わかるようにした。

7　a）　ここにごみをすてないようにください。
　　b）　　　　　　　　　　　なってください。
　　c）　　　　　　　　　　　してください。

8　a）　かぜをひかないように、頭が痛い。
　　b）　　　　　　　　　　　セーターを着る。
　　c）　　　　　　　　　　　あまり食べない。

Read the Grammar Notes of Lesson 22, and check how well you have understood it. Choose <u>the most appropriate statement.</u>

1　a）鈴木さんはガールフレンドを笑わせた。
　　b）　　　　　　　ガールフレンドに
　　c）　　　　　　　ガールフレンドが

2　a）先生はアニルさんを発表をさせた。
　　b）　　　　アニルさんに
　　c）　　　　アニルさんが

3　a）アニルさんは先生に手紙を書かせました。
　　b）　　　　　　　　　　　書いてくださいました。
　　c）　　　　　　　　　　　書いていただきました。

4　「弟に部屋をそうじさせました。」
　　Q：だれがそうじしましたか。
　　a）弟
　　b）私

5　「友だちにワープロを使わせてもらいました。」
　　Q：だれが使いましたか。
　　a）友だち
　　b）私

6　a）熱があるので、午後の授業を休んでいただけませんか。
　　b）　　　　　　　　　　　　　休ませていただけませんか。

7　a）田中さんはかぜだ　らしい。
　　b）　　　　　　かぜです
　　c）　　　　　　かぜ

8　a）忙しいじゃない　　と思って、電話しなかった。
　　b）忙しいじゃないか
　　c）忙しいんじゃない
　　d）忙しいんじゃないか

9　a）今月の給料はもう使っておきました。
　　b）　　　　　　　　　　　あります。
　　c）　　　　　　　　　　　しまいました。

文法（ぶんぽう）チェック L23

Read the Grammar Notes of Lesson 23, and check how well you have understood it.
Choose <u>the most appropriate statement.</u>

1   a)   今年論文を出しなければなりません。
     b)   出さなければ
     c)   出せなければ

2   A：大使館へ行かなければなりませんか。
     a)   B：いいえ、行かなければなりません。
     b)   行ってもいいです。
     c)   行かなくてもいいです。

3   a)   来年結婚する　ことにしました。
     b)   結婚するの
     c)   結婚した

4   a)   いま　　実験が終わったところです。
     b)   去年
     c)   いまから

5   A：いま何をしているんですか。
     a)   B：宿題をやる　　　ところです。
     b)   やっている
     c)   やった

6   a)   結婚するために、貯金している。   （貯金する *to save money*）
     b)   ように、

7   a)   かぜをひかないために、セーターを持っていく。
     b)   ように、

文法 (ぶんぽう) チェック L24

Read the Grammar Notes of Lesson 24, and check how well you have understood it. Choose the most appropriate statement.

1   a)   この本を読むのなら、貸してください。
    b)   貸しましょうか。

2   A：ちょっと郵便局へ行ってきます。
    a)   B：郵便局へ行ったら、この手紙を出してきてください。
    b)   行けば、
    c)   行くと、
    d)   行くなら、

3   a)   雨が降っても、行きません。
    b)   行きます。
    c)   行きました。

4   a)   いくらさがしても、見つかりませんでした。
    b)   見つかりました。

5   a)   たくさん食べたのに、おなかがすいています。
    b)   いっぱいです。

6   a)   コーヒーを飲む　のに、まだねむいです。
    b)   飲んだ

7   A：田中さんは、子どものとき、アメリカに住んでいたんです。
    a)   B：英語が上手　わけですね。
    b)   上手の
    c)   上手な

8   A：田中さんはいらっしゃいますか。
    a)   B：きょうは火曜日なので、午後来るつもりです。
    b)   わけ
    c)   はず

II. Answers to Grammar Check and Model Conversation Check

1. Answers to Grammar Check

L17	1. b	2. c	3. b	4. a	5. c	6. a	7. b	8. c	
L18	1. b	2. a	3. b,a	4. b	5. c	6. b	7. a	8. c	9. a
L19	1. b	2. c	3. c	4. b	5. a	6. b	7. a	8. a	9. b
L20	1. c	2. b	3. c	4. a	5. c	6. a	7. b	8. a	9. b
L21	1. a	2. b	3. c	4. c	5. b	6. a	7. c	8. b	
L22	1. a	2. b	3. c	4. a	5. b	6. b	7. c	8. d	9. c
L23	1. b	2. c	3. a	4. a	5. b	6. a	7. b		
L24	1. b	2. d	3. b	4. a	5. a	6. b	7. c	8. c	

2. Answers to Model Conversation Check

L17	I.	1. b	2. a	3. b	4. b	5. c
	II.	1. c	2. b	3. a	4. c	5. b
L18	I.	1. c	2. b	3. b	4. c	5. a
	II.	1. a	2. b	3. b	4. c	5. c
L19	I.	1. b	2. a	3. b	4. c	5. c
	II.	1. c	2. a	3. b	4. c	5. b
L20	I.	1. c	2. a	3. c	4. b	5. b
	II.	1. b	2. c	3. a	4. b	5. b
L21	I.	1. b	2. b	3. a	4. c	5. a
	II.	1. b	2. c	3. b	4. c	5. b
L22	I.	1. c	2. a	3. c	4. b	5. c
	II	1. b	2. a	3. c	4. b	5. c
L23	I.	1. b	2. b	3. c	4. b	5. b
	II.	1. c	2. a	3. b	4. a	5. c
L24	I.	1. c	2. a	3. b	4. b	5. c
	II.	1. b	2. c	3. b	4. a	5. c

Index to Grammar Notes (L17~L24)

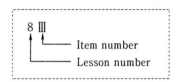

261

262

Index to Conversation Notes (L1〜L24)

Giving information

………です。	L1GI-3
………ではありません。	L2GI-3
………円いただきます。	L3GI-1a
………円のおかえしになります。	L3GI-2b
<thing>をお願いします。	L3S-3a
べつべつにしてください。	L3S-5
頭が痛いんです。	L9S-1
まっすぐ行ってください。	L12S-1
まっすぐ行って、右に曲がってください。	
〜て、<location>です。	
〜と、<location>にあります。	
<shape/colour/size etc.>です。	L14S-4
<landmark>の近くなんですけど。	L15S-5
私、松見大学の山下ともうしますが。	L18S-1

Confirming information

………ですか。／………ですね。	L4S-4ab
事務室って、宿舎の事務室ですか。	L5S-3
52の3181じゃありませんか。	L7S-3
右に曲がると、歩道橋があります。	L12S-3
―右に曲がるんですね。↗	
〜んだって。↗／ですって。↗	L13S-2
〜ですか。／ですね。↗	L14S-3

Saying something is correct

はい。／ええ。／うん。	L1GI-3

Saying something is not correct

いいえ。	L1GI-3
あのう、おつり、ちがっているんですけど。	L2GI-3c
あのう、これちがっているんですけど。	L3S-4c
いいえ、ちがいます。	L7S-3

Correcting someone

ここですか。 ―いや、そこじゃなくて、こっち。	L6S-3
いいえ、ちがいます。うちは山田ですけど。	L7S-3

Reporting something

事務室に取りにきてくださいって。	まとめ2BII5b
<time>ごろ、<person>から電話がありました。	
<message>と言ってました。	L18S-6

Explaing a procedure

まず／はじめに、……。次に、……	L20S-2

Judgement

Asking for advice implicitly
　　ええと、はんこはもっていないんですけど。　　　　　　　　　　　　L6S-4

Asking for permission
　　＜Reason＞んです。 ｜ ～てもよろしいでしょうか。　　　　　　　L8S-3a
　　　　　　　んで。 ｜ [V]たいんですが。
　　～ても／～なくてもいいでしょうか。　　　　　　　　　　　　　　L9S-2

Asking for someone's judgement
　　[N] は私には、[A/NA] でしょうか。　　　　　　　　　　　　　　L10S-2
　　[N１] と [N２] とどちらがいいでしょうか。　　　　　　　　　　L10S-2
　　＜group＞の中でどれが一番いいかな。　　　　　　　　　　　　　　L10S-2

Giving reasons
　　|S１| ｜ ものですから ｜ 、|S２|　　　　　　　　　　　　　　　L13S-1
　　　　 ｜ ので ｜
　　仕事も終わったし、おなかもすいたし、　　　　　　　　　　　　　L16S-1

Expressing opinion
　　～んじゃない。↗／～じゃないでしょうか。↗　　　　　　　　　　L20S-4
　　[N]がいい。／いいと思う。　　　　　　　　　　　　　　　　　　L24S-1

Making a proposal
　　～たほうがいいんじゃないでしょうか。＜reason＞ ｜ から。　　　L24S-1
　　　　　　　　　　　　　　　　　　　　　　　　 ｜ いし。

Asking the others' opinion
　　[N]はどう。↗／どうですか。　　　　　　　　　　　　　　　　　L24S-1

Giving an opposite view
　　でも／しかし、～と思うんですが。／反対です。　　　　　　　　　L24S-2

Supporting someone's view
　　そうですね。いい考えだと思います。　　　　　　　　　　　　　　L24S-3

Asking someone's approval
　　そうでしょう。↗／そう思いません。↗／いかがですか。　　　　　L24S-4

Evading a definite statement
　　ええ、まあ／はあ　　　　　　　　　　　　　　　　　　　　　　L24S-4

Actions

Offering to do something for someone
　　[N]と呼んでください。　　　　　　　　　　　　　　　　　　　　L1S-2b
　　これ、おねがいします。　　　　　　　　　　　　　　　　　　　　L2S-1a
　　＜thing＞を＜number＞ ｜ お願いします。　　　　　　　　　　　L2S-4
　　　　　　　　　　　　　 ｜ ください。
　　これでおねがいします。　　　　　　　　　　　　　　　　　　　　L2GI-3a
　　こちらへどうぞ。　　　　　　　　　　　　　　　　　　　　　　　L3GI-2a
　　もう少し待ってください。　　　　　　　　　　　　　　　　　　　L3S-4a

<action verb>てください。 L6GI-1
[N]の電話番号教えてください。 L7S-1a
<shape/colour/size>の［N］を見せてください。 L10S-1
注文お願いします。 L11S-2
悪いんですけど、注文取り消してください。 L11S-3
～てあげてもいいよ。／～てあげてもいいよ。 L13S-3
タクシー呼ぼうか。／呼びましょうか。 L16S-1
<place>までお願いします。 L16S-3
<place>を～に曲がってください。 L16S-5
<place>で止めてください。 L16S-5
<time>ごろ、またお電話します。 L18S-3
伝言お願いします。 L18S-4
<message>とお伝えください。 L18S-5
～てもらえる。↗／～てもらえないかな。 L20S-3
ちょっと手伝ってもらえないかな。 L23S-2

Giving something
はい。 L2S-1
どうぞ。 L3S-2
つまらないものですが。 L19S-2
あの、これ、お見舞い。 L22S-2

Receiving something
あ、どうも。 L3S-2
よろしいんですか。／じゃ、えんりょなく。 L13S-4

Asking for instructions
………が分からないんですけど。 L6S-2a

Checking what you have done
これでいいですか。 L6S-2b

Asking for permission
あの、………で(も)いいですか。 L6S-5b
<reason>んです。……てもよろしいでしょうか。 L8S-3a
<reason>んです。～[V]-たいんですが。／ですけど。 L8S-3a
～ても／～なくてもいいでしょうか。 L9S-2
もう一度、お電話してもよろしいでしょうか。 L18S-3

Giving permission
いいですよ。／かまいませんよ。 L8S-3c

Refusing permission
～[V]ではだめです。／いけません。 L8S-3c
～[V]ないでください。 L8S-3c

Asking for advice
ええと、はんこもってないんですけど。 L6S-4
～について何かありませんか。 L15S-1

Giving an alternative
じゃ、………でもいいです。／けっこうです。 L6S-5a
そう。じゃ日曜はどう。↗ L17S-3a

Warning someone
～Vないでください。 L8S-4a

気をつけてください。／注意してください。／忘れないで。 　　　　　L22S-5

Suggesting
　　じゃ、………はどう。↗／どうですか。 　　　　　　　　　　　　　L6S-5a

Enquireing for something
　　〜に忘れものしたんですが、〜ていただけませんか。 　　　　　　　L14S-1

Making an appointment
　　じゃ、<time/date>にお願いします。 　　　　　　　　　　　　　　L7S-6a
　　いつがよろしいでしょうか。 　　　　　　　　　　　　　　　　　　L7S-6b
　　<time/date>は、どうでしょうか。 　　　　　　　　　　　　　　　L7S-6c

Inviting someone
　　あした、映画に行きませんか。／お時間ありますか。／来ませんか。 　L17S-1a

Declining an invitation
　　土曜は、ちょっと。／いいえ、だめなんです。／申し訳けありません。 　L17S-3a

Calling someone on the phone
　　田中みどりさん、おねがいします。 　　　　　　　　　　　　　　　L18S-2

Making a request
　　すみませんが[V]ていただけませんか。／もらえませんか。 　　　　L23S-2

Refusing a request
　　申しわけありませんが、ちょっと。 　　　　　　　　　　　　　　　L23S-3

Withdrawing a request
　　すみませんが、ちょっと……。 　　　　　　　　　　　　　　　　　L23S-4
　　悪いけど、いま、ちょっと忙しいんだ。 　　　　　　　　　　　　　L23S-4

Persuading someone
　　そこを何とか、おねがいします。 　　　　　　　　　　　　　　　　L23S-5

Social formulas

Introducing yourself
　　はじめまして。[N]ともうします。／です。
　　どうぞよろしくお願いします。 　　　　　　　　　　　　　　　　　L1GI-1a

Introducing someone
　　こちら、[N]さんです。 　　　　　　　　　　　　　　　　　　　　L1S-2b

Reaching an introduction
　　[N]です。よろしくお願いします。 　　　　　　　　　　　　　　　L1S-2b

Starting a conversation
　　あのう、失礼ですが。 　　　　　　　　　　　　　　　　　　　　　L1GI-2b
　　どちらへ。／どこ行くの。 　　　　　　　　　　　　　　　　　　　L2S-1a
　　すみません。 　　　　　　　　　　　　　　　　　　　　　　　　　L2S-2
　　失礼します。 　　　　　　　　　　　　　　　　　　　　　　　　　L8S-1a
　　ちょっとよろしいでしょうか。 　　　　　　　　　　　　　　　　　L8S-1b

Expressing politeness
　　お／ご[N] 　　　　　　　　　　　　　　　　　　　　　　　　　　L1GI-1b

Expressing modesty
　　いいえ、そんなことないですよ。／それほどでも。 　　　　　　　　L13S-5

Greetings

こんにちは。／おはようございます。／こんばんは。	L18-1
いらっしゃいませ。	L3GI-2a
ひさしぶりですね。／しばらく。／ごぶさたしています。	L15S-1
おじゃまします。／おじゃましました。	L19S-1
ごちそうさまでした。	L19S-3b

Talking about how one's getting on

どうですか。／いかがですか。	L15S-1
ーおかげさまで。／なんとか。	

Talking about others

～さんは、どうしていますか。	L15S-2

Thanking

どうも。／ごちそうさまでした。	3S-5b
ありがとうございます。	まとめ1BII4
——いいえ、どういたしまして。	
どうもすみません。	まとめ1BII4c
すみません。お手数をかけて。	L15S-3
今日は、本当にありがとうございました。	L19S-4
ご心配いただいて、ありがとうございます。	L22S-2a

Apologizing

すみません。まちがえました。	L7S-3
＜reason＞て、ごめん。／すみません。／申し訳ありません。	L13S-4
すみません。これから気をつけます。	L21S-3
ごめん。気がつかなくて。／悪い。	L21S-4

Declining politely

ううん………／ちょっと。～のほうがいいんですけど。	L10S-3

Emotion

Embarrassment

ううん………。↘／さあ………。↘	L5S-4

Praising

わあ。おいしそうですね。	L19S-2

Pleasure

きょうは、とっても楽しかったです。	L19S-3c

Complaint

あのう。申しわけありませんが、テレビの音が。	L21S-1

Anger

頭に来る／いいかげんにしてよ。／冗談いわないでよ。	L21S-2

Encouragement

心配しなくても、大丈夫ですよ。	
すぐ元気になりますよ。／がんばって。	L22S-4

Condolence

このたびはどうも。／どうかあまり力をおとされないように。	L22GI-2a

Celebration

おめでとうございます。 L22GI-2b

Sympathy

大変でしたね。 L22S-1

Communication strategies

Getting someone's attention

あ(ああ)／あら まとめ1BII3a

あ(あのう) まとめ1BII3b

Aizuchi

はい。／ええ。／そうですね。／そうですか。／なるほど。 L1GI-4

Starting a conversation

あ、[N]さん。こんにちは。 L1S-1

ちょっと。／ちょっと、すみません。 L1S-1c

どちらへ。／どこ行くの。 L2S-1

すみません。／お願いします。 L2S-2

あの、ちょっとすみません。 L4S-1

あの、ちょっとうかがいますが。 L4S-1

もしもし。 L7S-2

あの、ちょっとおたずねしたいんですが。 L7S-4

(knock-knock)失礼します。

ちょっとよろしいでしょうか。 L8S-1

何してんの。／しているんですか。／どうしたの。 L20S-1

Ending a conversation

それじゃ、また。／じゃ。 L1S-3a

さようなら。 L1S-3b

じゃ、失礼します。 L2S-3c

ちょっと、そこまで。

どうも｜ありがとうございました。 L4S-6a
　　　｜すみませんでした。

じゃ、いいです。 L5S-5

失礼します。／ごめんください。／じゃ、また。 L18S-5

じゃ、よろしくお願いします。 L7S-6d

もう、そろそろ失礼します。 L19S-4

Introducing a main topic

掲示板にこれがはってあったんですけど。 L5S-1/L6S-1

………のことなんですが。／けど。実は、 L8S-2

Changing the topic

ところで、＜the main topic＞ L13S-2

Summing up

じゃ、コーヒーふたつ、紅茶ひとつください。 L3S-3c

Saying something again

すみません、もういちどお願いします。 L4S-3a

Compiled and Edited by:

General editor	Otsubo, Kazuo	大 坪 一 夫
Authors	Akutsu, Satoru	阿久津　　智
	Ichikawa, Yasuko	市 川 保 子
	Emura, Hirofumi	江 村 裕 文
	Ogawa, Taeko	小 川 多恵子
	Kano, Chieko	加 納 千恵子
	Kaiser, Stefan	カイザー シュテファン
	Kindaichi, Kyoko	金田一 京 子
	Kobayashi, Noriko	小 林 典 子
	Komiya, Shutaro	小 宮 修太郎
	Saegusa, Reiko	三 枝 令 子
	Sakai, Takako	酒 井 たか子
	Shimizu, Yuri	清 水 百 合
	Shinya, Ayuri	新 谷 あゆり
	Tochigi, Yuka	栃 木 由 香
	Tomura, Kayo	戸 村 佳 代
	Nishimura, Yoshimi	西 村 よしみ
	Hashimoto, Yoji	橋 本 洋 二
	Fujimaki, Kikuko	藤 牧 喜久子
	Ford, Junko	フォード 順子
	Homma, Tomoko	本 間 倫 子
	Yamamoto, Sonoko	山 本 そのこ
	Yokoyama, Noriko	横 山 紀 子
	Watanabe, Keiko	渡 辺 恵 子
Cover design	Robles, Maria Elizabeth	ロブレスM.エリザベス
Illustrator	Teshigahara, Midori	勅使河原　緑

SITUATIONAL FUNCTIONAL JAPANESE
VOLUME THREE: NOTES

1992年3月15日　　初　版第1刷発行
1997年2月28日　　第2版第2刷発行

著　者　　筑波ランゲージグループ
発行所　　株式会社　凡 人 社
〒102 東京都千代田区平河町1－3－13
菱進平河町ビル1F　電話 03－3472－2240